† John Serlei Hapin

One Faith and Fellowship

One Faith

and Fellowship

THE MISSIONARY STORY OF THE ANGLICAN COMMUNION

JOHN SEVILLE HIGGINS
Bishop of Rhode Island

Foreword by
THE ARCHBISHOP OF
CANTERBURY

GREENWICH · CONNECTICUT · 1958

TO

MARION, JOHN, and ANNE

WITH LOVE

Foreword

After the isolation of the war years, the 1948 Lambeth Conference brought a fresh sense of unity and purpose to the Bishops of the Anglican Communion. The great Anglican Congress of 1954 did for us all, clergy and laity, what Lambeth had begun for the Bishops. The Bishops who come to the 1958 Conference are limited this time in number to about 300 so that we may keep the intimacy and fruitfulness of discussion which larger numbers imperil. They will come better known to one another and more conscious of their fellowship and responsibility in the Anglican Communion than was possible before. They will take up again consideration of the problems which always face the Church but are always presenting new aspects and new perplexities and new challenges and hopes—what the Holy Spirit is at this time saying to us from the Holy Bible about the unity of the Church, about the Anglican contribution to its total witness, about inter-racial and international conflicts, about the family in the midst of social change.

But Christ was confronting his Church with these same problems ever since St. Augustine came to Canterbury, ever since the Church of England found itself expanding to countries and races overseas owing to emigrants and merchants and colonists and missionaries. You will not understand all the riches and problems of the Anglican Communion today unless you know something of its history from the first Archbishop of Canterbury of 597 to the ninety-ninth of 1957. It is a fascinating and exhilarating story, the same faith and the same problems and each successive answer to them of faithful men. Here is the story told for you to read and admire—and to continue to the Glory of God.

GEOFFREY CANTUAR:

Preface

The purpose of these pages is to give an outline of the development of the Church of England into the world-wide Anglican Communion; the assignment was undertaken at the request of the Anglican Sub-Committee of the Joint Commission on Ecumenical Relations of the Episcopal Church.

The Right Reverend Lauriston L. Scaife, Bishop of Western New York and Chairman of the Anglican Sub-Committee, has both given the project much encouragement and also has provided a subsidy for the inclusion of the maps. The latter were drawn by Miss Norma Lord from outlines and illustrative material supplied by the author.

I am indebted particularly to Canon Howard A. Johnson, and to the Reverend Professors Edward R. Hardy and Powel M. Dawley for reading the manuscript and giving their scholarly advice. Mrs. Anita M. Downes, the author's secretary, has been of immense help and an indispensable colleague.

The book makes no claim to original scholarship or research, but it is hoped that those who read it will catch a glimpse of the devoted labors and the Christian statesmanship, as well as the heroisms and the martyrdoms, of a great host of Anglican clergy and laypeople who have taken the Faith as this Church has received the same to the far corners of the earth.

JOHN SEVILLE HIGGINS

The Bishop's House
Providence, Rhode Island

Contents

xiii

List of Pictorial Maps

CHAPTER ONE

The British Isles

The British Isles

THE CHURCH OF ENGLAND

As the Gospel of Jesus Christ spread beyond the confines of the Jerusalem Church throughout the Mediterranean world and northward through Gaul, traders and soldiers, converted to the new faith, reached the shores of England. The year 175 can be fixed as the approximate time of the first encounter of the English with Christianity; and the Church of England has borne unbroken witness to the apostolic faith since these first Christian missionaries came to Britain. Thus she can claim to be the true Catholic Church of the land.

Although there are few certain dates in this early era, we do know that records show the presence of three British bishops at the Council of Arles, in Gaul, in 314. During the latter years of the fourth century the Roman legions, which had occupied the country since the last decades of the first century, were gradually withdrawn and finally left completely in 409. This left Britain exposed, and not long after there began a series of devastating invasions by the pagan Jutes, Angles, and Saxons which ravaged the nation and extinguished Christianity in the south for the next 150 years. The defeated natives fled west and north, taking their faith with them; and by the year 600 all of England was firmly under the rule of the heathen Saxon conquerors.

The evangelization of Britain had now to begin all over

3

again, and the missionaries who undertook the task came from three directions: Iona, Rome, and Northumbria. St. Columba, a young Irish monk, crossed to Scotland in 563, where he founded an Irish, or Celtic, missionary center on the Isle of Iona. This group formed a spearhead of missionary advance on Britain from the northwest. In 597 St. Augustine, a Roman monk, under orders from Pope Gregory I, landed in Kent to begin missionary work from the South. Another Celt, St. Aidan, established a monastery at Lindisfarne just off the Northumberland coast of England in 635, which also became a notable and effective center of Christian life and work.

St. Augustine, who became the first Archbishop of Canterbury late in 597, was not able to secure the cooperation of the British bishops of the old, pre-invasion Church in the west, who regarded him as an intruder. However, after Augustine's death the British and Roman missionaries reached an agreement at the Council of Whitby in 664. A succeeding Archbishop of Canterbury, Theodore of Tarsus (668-690), through his administrative genius was able to erect fourteen territorial dioceses covering the whole area of the Saxon occupation.

Disaster struck Britain again in 793 when the Danish invasion that lasted until 871 quite thoroughly smashed the Church and much of Britain's civilization. It was not until the year 878 that King Alfred defeated the Danes and imposed upon them the Treaty of Wedmore, whereby they drew back north of the Thames and left Alfred in possession of Wessex. This latter kingdom was a center from which the Christian faith again spread over the land. In 973 England became a nation when Edgar was crowned king of all England by the Archbishop of Canterbury. Except for

Canute's short-lived, dual empire, this Saxon line of kings continued to rule the land until King Harold died at Hastings in 1066, in the battle against the Normans.

The successful invasion of Britain by William of Normandy brought vast changes to that land, in the course of which the Church lost its insular character and became more closely linked with the Church on the Continent. Norman clergy took over most of the important clerical posts. Eager to create a precedent, Pope Gregory VII demanded that William receive the Crown of England as a fief from his hands and do homage to him; but this William stoutly refused to do since, as he rightly said, no former English king had done so.

The five centuries which intervened between the Norman Conquest and the Reformation witnessed a continuing struggle between the Crown and the Papacy for control of the Church of England. These years are, in good part, the story of Anselm against William II and Henry I; of Becket against Henry II; and of Langton against King John. During these centuries, the power and pretensions of the Papacy increased steadily, for the popes laid claim to supreme authority over both Church and State. The political alliances of successive popes with varying combinations of states caused serious corruption both to the Papacy and the papal court, while the Great Schism of the fourteenth century culminated in the distressing spectacle of no fewer than three rival popes! The need for reform became increasingly apparent, and in the first half of the fifteenth century there began a movement seeking to make the General Councils, and not the Pope, the supreme authority in the Church. This would have been much more in accord with the primitive and apostolic practice of the Church, but the movement was defeated when, in 1460, the principle of conciliar supremacy was condemned by Pius II, who thereby made inevitable a reformation by revolution.

The Reformation of the sixteenth century affected the whole of Europe. In the German States and Switzerland radical reforms in both faith and practice were made. England, on the other hand, carried through a more conservative type of reformation, one that was in essence a rejection of the papal system and a retention of the ancient and Catholic faith. Over the centuries England had protested the ever-increasing papal taxation and claims, but the spark which finally ignited the flame for reform in England was Henry the Eighth's marital problems, the "King's Matter" as it was called.

Seventeen years of Henry's marriage to Catherine of Aragon, his dead brother's widow, had failed to produce a male heir to the throne. This raised serious problems for the Tudor dynasty and the nation. Therefore, Henry appealed to the Pope for an annulment of the marriage. This was not an unusual request; various popes had granted annulments upon a number of occasions. For instance, Henry's sister, Margaret of Scotland, had had her previous marriage annulled and had married the divorced Louis XI of France in 1514. A year after Louis died, she married the divorced Duke of Suffolk. And Henry's request was partially based on the canon law of the medieval church which forbade an "in-law" marriage, although Pope Julius had set aside this law to permit Henry's marriage to Catherine in the first place. But Pope Clement hesitated to nullify his predecessor's dispensation and the matter dragged on for four years. The Pope's refusal to grant Henry's request was not due to Christian principles, but to the fact that the powerful Holy

6

Roman Emperor, Charles V, was the nephew of Queen Catherine of England. Also the political relationship between the papacy and the Empire was such that the Pope did not dare to speak his mind, with imperial troops occupying the city of Rome.

Henry finally lost patience, married Anne Boleyn secretly, forbade any and all appeals to Rome, made himself Supreme Head of the Church of England, and got the consent of the Archbishop of Canterbury, Thomas Cranmer, to the annulment of his previous marriage.

It should be remembered that Henry's personal conduct in no way affected the continuity of the Church, for the clergy continued to exercise their ministry and the people continued to receive the sacraments as they had before the break with Rome. No specific date can, therefore, be assigned for the "founding" of the Church of England during the Reformation, for the precise reason that it was in fact continuous with the Church that preceded it.

Brilliant though he was, there is little doubt that Henry was a wicked man. This can also be said of many of the popes of that day. But the catholicity of the Church of England was not destroyed by Henry's conduct any more than the wickedness of individual popes destroyed the Catholic faith. We must remember, too, that Henry was a product of his age; and while this does not excuse him, his conduct and character must be considered in the total picture of the times in which he lived. It can be said that, as a political theorist and as a lay theologian, Henry VIII ranked very high. And it may be that these two accomplishments led him to see himself in the dual role of the Emperor Justinian of the 6th century. Whatever Henry's real motives were, both Church and nation were consolidated under his reign, and

England's face was turned in the direction of national greatness.

One of the universal results of the Reformation was the translation of church services into a tongue understood by the people. In England under Henry this desire for a native language liturgy led to the publication, in 1549, of the Book of Common Prayer, largely the work of Thomas Cranmer.

Henry was succeeded by his only son, young Edward VI, who ruled briefly through a regency. Then came Mary, daughter of Henry VIII and Catherine of Aragon, who brought England back to the papal fold for the five years of her unhappy reign. Her marriage to Philip II of Spain gave England no comfort, and the sobriquet "Bloody Mary" was the just result of the bigotry which caused her to persecute and kill many adherents to the reformed faith. Bishops Latimer and Ridley, and finally Archbishop Cranmer and many others were burned at the stake for heresy during Mary's short reign.

In 1558 Elizabeth I, daughter of Henry VIII and Anne Boleyn, followed Mary to the throne, and the reformed faith was re-established. With the Pope's special blessing, Philip II of Spain despatched the Armada to recapture England for Rome; but its disastrous defeat stopped the threat of invasion, impressed the continent with the solidarity of England, and initiated an era of prosperity and peace. Elizabeth's one aim during her long reign was to bring peace to the land, and in this she largely succeeded. While plans to assassinate her brought immediate reprisals, her reign was free from the cruel excesses of her sister, Mary Tudor. And the execution of the immoral and feckless Mary Queen of

Scots came about precisely because she was deeply implicated in the assassination plots against Elizabeth in order that she might return to the throne and bring papal power with her.

It is interesting to note that seven popes ruled in Rome between 1534 and 1570 before Pius V excommunicated Elizabeth for heresy and released her subjects from their allegiance to her. While this act was of serious and pathetic consequence for Roman Catholics in England, it did complete the break made by Henry VIII thirty-five years before, and left no hope for reconciliation.

Elizabeth's great reign ended in 1603 and was followed by the Stuart period which, except for the eleven years of Cromwell's Commonwealth, lasted until 1688. James VI of Scotland, who now became James I of England, decided to stand with the Established Church against the growing power of the Puritan element who were sure that the Reformation had not gone nearly far enough and who wanted the Church of England to follow Calvin's Genevan model. His successor, Charles I, was a thorough Anglican and a man of impeccable personal life. However, he was quite convinced that his kingship came by divine right, and that he should be an absolute ruler. This unfortunate point of view necessarily caused the King to regard Parliament as his creature, a circumstance that brought about increasing tension, culminating in the execution of Archbishop William Laud, then civil war, and finally the execution of the King himself in 1649.

The successful rebellion of the Puritans against Charles and the Church saw the establishment of the Commonwealth under Oliver Cromwell. Bishops, clergy, Prayer Book, and the Established Church gave way to a presbyterian system for a while. But when Cromwell died England was ready to welcome the third Stuart, Charles II, to the throne, and to renew the Establishment.* Bishops and clergy were reinstated, and a revised Prayer Book issued in 1662. The last of the Stuarts, James II, made an attempt to reintroduce the Roman faith, an attempt which cost him his throne in 1688, when William and Mary became joint sovereigns. The events of the previous century and a half had made it clear that England wanted an English Church for the English people. The great divines who had lived during the seventeenth century—Richard Hooker, Lancelot Andrewes, Jeremy Taylor, George Herbert, and Nicholas Ferrar to mention but a few—did much by their personal sanctity and scholarship to erect the firm foundation for Anglicanism, a foundation which held against the extremes of Rome on the one side, and Geneva on the other, and which defined the Church's position as a *via media* between them.

The first quarter of the eighteenth century was a particularly fortunate time for the Church of England, and it is probable that not more than five per cent of the people of England were outside its fold in the year 1700. It was in this period also that the Church began to think of her responsibilities elsewhere than in England, particularly in the mission field of the colonies. However, the general level of religious life declined as the century wore on, in spite of the fact that notable individuals such as Joseph Butler, George Berkeley,

---

*The Church of England is an "Established Church," a word first used in this connection in 1604. It does not mean that the Church was at any time established or set up by statute, but rather that the Church is the official representative of the State in matters of religion. The Sovereign, who must be in communion with the Church, nominates to all bishoprics and deaneries and to some other Church offices; Convocation cannot enact canons without the Royal Assent; and Church courts are in some ways subject to secular courts.

William Law, and Samuel Johnson continued to star the Anglican firmament. Since Convocation had been silenced by Parliament from 1717—because of violent disputes among its members—the Church had no corporate voice, but had to rely on certain of its bishops who were in the House of Lords to make known the needs of the Church. Convocation was finally restored in 1854, but the long lapse had done great harm.

The vigor of the Church of England was likewise weakened by the strong Methodist movement which, while it began within the Church, finally broke away and took great numbers of the new middle class with it. However, there was a stirring by the Holy Spirit in all this, for towards the end of the eighteenth century the Evangelical Movement began; and as it gathered momentum it quickened the conscience of England. It was largely responsible for the eventual abolition of the slave trade, and it provided the impetus for a vast missionary expansion overseas. The great figures of the Evangelical Revival placed their emphasis on preaching and individual conversions, but had little to say about Church order and sacraments. This had the result of obscuring in the minds of the laity and general clergy, the historical and catholic heritage of the Church, and it caused an imbalance that was detrimental to careful and orderly liturgical practice and study. The corrective to this was administered by the Oxford Movement which began in 1833. This movement had for its object the restoration of the full Catholic faith and worship in the Church, and it was led by three priests of the Church of England, Keble, Pusey and Newman (the latter finally went to Rome). The message of this Catholic revival was that nothing in the Church's faith and formularies was at essential variance with the Catholic faith of the ages.

11

A notable succession of parish priests, among them Fathers Dolling, Tooth, and Staunton taught the faith, worked with the poor, and endured the unremitting attacks of the Evangelicals who feared that the Oxford Movement would lead the Church back to Rome.

The new vigor of the Church became apparent in the erection of the new diocese of Ripon in 1836, the first new bishopric since the Reformation; it was followed by seven more new dioceses before the end of the century and eleven more have been added since 1900. The social thinking of the Church received great impetus through the life and writings of Frederick Denison Maurice, whose book *The Kingdom of Christ* became the foundation of the Christian Socialist movement. The intellectual vigor of the Church was manifested, also, in her scholars of the new age who strove to accommodate the faith to the inroads of scientific thought and the new biblical criticism of continental scholars.

The Church of England consists of two provinces, Canterbury and York, and each of the Convocations consists of two Houses, an Upper House and a Lower House. The Upper House is made up of the diocesan bishops of the Province and is presided over by its Archbishop. The Lower House has for its members elected members of the clergy (called proctors) and some ex-officio members. It will be noted that Convocation is solely a clerical body; the laity are given a voice in the National Assembly of the Church of England, called the Church Assembly, which meets at least once a year. This consists of three Houses: The House of Bishops, which is made up from the members of the Upper Houses of the two Convocations; The House of Clergy, which consists of the members of the Lower Houses of the two Convocations;

and The House of Laity. These latter are the elected lay representatives of the two provinces together with some ten co-opted members. Because of the Establishment, there is a Parliamentary Ecclesiastical Committee of thirty persons, fifteen from Lords nominated by the Lord Chancellor, and fifteen from Commons nominated by the Speaker. It is this Committee which initiates ecclesiastical legislation in Parliament.

In modern times the Church of England has had a continuing interest in the reunion of Christendom, and it has made valuable contributions to the whole ecumenical movement. Progress with the Roman Church has been generally unproductive, due largely to the fact that a little over a century ago (1850) the Roman hierarchy was established in England soon after the Roman Catholic Emancipation Act of 1829. A devout Anglican, Lord Halifax, and the Abbé Portal, a French Roman Catholic, made an unofficial attempt towards the end of the nineteenth century to get Pope Leo XIII to declare the validity of Anglican orders as a first step towards a better understanding between Rome and Canterbury. Not unexpectedly, the hopes of the two men and others were dashed when, in 1896, the Pope issued the bull *Apostolicae Curae,* which stated flatly that Anglican orders were null and void. The reasons given in the bull for the decision were so flimsy that Archbishop of Canterbury Benson, after he had duly read the bull, wrote his brother Maclagan of York, ". . . we are surer than ever before, now we know Leo XIII's reasons, that they have nothing to say." [1] The Archbishops wrote a devastating reply to the bull which was given wide distribution.

After World War I a distinguished group of Roman Catholics and Anglicans, inspired by the great and saintly Désiré

13

Cardinal Mercier, held a series of conversations at Malines. These "Malines Conversations" were finally terminated by the Pope, but they did serve to show that some Roman Catholics and some Anglicans hold much of the Faith in common.

More success has attended the Church of England in her approaches to other Christian communions. A measure of intercommunion was achieved with the Swedish National Church in 1920, and in 1934 full intercommunion took place with the Old Catholics, who had broken from Rome in 1870 over the question of papal infallibility. The Orthodox Churches of Jerusalem, Cyprus, Constantinople, and Roumania declared Anglican orders valid in the period between the two world wars, and these were important steps towards a better understanding with these Churches.[2]

Various approaches have been made to the Free Churches, notably the "Appeal to All Christian Peoples" issued by the Lambeth Conference of 1920. While there is a high degree of cooperation between the Church of England and the Free Churches, there has yet been no great advance towards reunion.

Certainly there are some needed reforms in the present relationship of the Church and the State, particularly in the matters of episcopal elections and Prayer Book revision. The Church must exercise her right to choose her own bishops rather than have them chosen by the Prime Minister. Actually there is close consultation in the nomination of bishops between the Prime Minister and the Archbishop of Canterbury. However this is not mandatory and if it were, the Church must still have the right to choose her own leaders.

The Church must also have full control over her own

worship, which she does not have at present, for the refusal of Parliament to allow a revision of the Prayer Book in 1928 pointed up an intolerable situation for the Church. A much-needed revision of Canon Law was presented to the Convocations in 1957: it represents the first revision since the early seventeenth century. There is also need to replace the present Judicial Committee of the Privy Council with another body made up of Churchmen. At present the Judicial Committee is the highest ecclesiastical court in the land, but its personnel do not have to be members of the Church of England. Under these circumstances it is understandable that clergy and laymen are unwilling to accept the Committee's ecclesiastical judgments. These reforms and others will doubtless take place in the course of time, and so perhaps make disestablishment unnecessary.

A remarkable feature of the Church of England has been its major contributions to scholarship, particularly in the fields of the Holy Scriptures, Church History and Liturgics. Without question she has led the way for her daughter Churches in this regard. A major weakness in the practical sphere has been her seeming inability to teach her members that they must give proper financial support to the Church of which they are members, and not rely on the inadequate stipends from "livings" to take care of their clergy.

A recent survey showed that sixty-seven out of every hundred children born in England are baptized at parish churches, but that only twenty-six are subsequently confirmed. This is due in great measure to the shortage of clergy and to the general dislocation of family life during and after two world wars. In spite of these adverse factors the Mother Church of Anglicanism is vigorous, increasingly sure of her position, and ready to share her treasure with those who will take the time to understand and value them as indispensable parts of the Church Catholic.

HOW THE ANGLICAN COMMUNION CAME TO BE

The Anglican Communion is a "Fellowship within the One, Holy, Catholic, and Apostolic Church, of those duly constituted dioceses, provinces, or regional Churches in communion with the See of Canterbury." These Churches are bound together by their desire to "uphold and propagate the Catholic and Apostolic faith and order as set forth in the Book of Common Prayer" and they are "national Churches bound together, not by a central legislative and executive authority, but by the mutual loyalty sustained through the common counsel of the bishops in conference." [3]

This worldwide expression of the ancient and Catholic faith consists today of fifteen self-governing Churches in the following countries and areas: England; Wales; Scotland; Ireland; Canada; the United States; the West Indies; South Africa; West Africa; Central Africa; India, Pakistan, Burma, and Ceylon; China; Japan; Australia and Tasmania; and New Zealand. Included also in the Anglican Communion are groups of dioceses contiguous to one another which are in various degrees moving towards provincial status. There are in addition certain dioceses and areas which are unlikely to be incorporated into provinces in the measurable future. The three hundred thirty-one dioceses which currently constitute the Anglican Communion cover a wide area of the globe as well as a long period of Christian history, for the diocese of London was founded before the year 314, while the latest

16

missionary district, Central America, was founded in 1956, a span of more than sixteen hundred and forty-two years.

START At the time of the Reformation there was no idea of an Anglican Communion; all that the English reformers did was to free their ancient Church from the Papacy, to acknowledge the Royal supremacy, and to produce the Book of Common Prayer. Indeed, there was no assurance that the reformed Church would continue to exist until the excommunication of Elizabeth in 1570 and the failure of the papal attempt to recapture England with the help of the Spanish Armada in 1588.

In speaking of the growth of the British Empire since the days of Queen Elizabeth I, Sir John Seeley once made the now famous statement that the English "seem, as it were, to have conquered and peopled half the world in a fit of absence of mind." [4] Bishop Alfred Barry rightly pointed out that what was true of the political expansion of England had its counterpart also in its ecclesiastical expansion: there was no long-range planning in either case. England's preoccupation with the aftermath of the Reformation, with the Stuart threat of arbitrary kingship, and with Cromwell, meant that it had no time or thought until after the Restoration of 1660 for its ecclesiastical responsibilities beyond the seas.

These responsibilities were beginning to be appreciable, for the Colonies in America were flourishing and the East India Company was opening up trade with the East. Englishmen were commencing to go all over the world, and they took with them their Anglican faith and their Book of Common Prayer. A nod in the direction of Christian responsibility for overseas developments was made by the Government in 1633 when, by an Order in Council, the Bishop of London was given spiritual jurisdiction for the American and other colonies. The effectiveness of this oversight depended naturally upon the ability and vision of the incumbents of that most ancient see; but Henry Compton, Bishop of London from 1675 to 1713, took a great interest in the affairs of the Colonial Church in America, and his personal interest was greatly responsible for awaking English church people to the religious needs of the Colonies.

Another small but significant indication that the Church of England was becoming aware of its larger responsibilities is indicated in the Preface to the new service of Holy Baptism for adults in the revised Prayer Book of 1662. It says in part concerning the service that it "may be always useful for the baptising of natives in our plantations and others converted to the faith." [5]

The "natives in our plantations and others" were greatly helped by the founding of two missionary societies which were destined to have a revolutionary effect on the Church of England. It must be remembered that the Convocation of the Church was silenced from 1717 to 1852, so that during those significant years the Church had no corporate voice. The suppression of Convocation made the great Dr. Samuel Johnson so enormously angry that he growled to Boswell: "Shall the Presbyterian Church of Scotland have its General Assembly and the Church of England be denied its Convocation?" [6] The answer, notwithstanding Dr. Johnson, was "Yes."

The missionary societies did make up in some degree for the Church's lack of corporate voice. The Society for Promoting Christian Knowledge (S.P.C.K.), when founded in 1698, was formed with the original purpose of giving Bibles and other edifying books to the poor of England; after a

18

few years it concerned itself with providing lending libraries of Christian books for the American colonists, and then to colonists elsewhere. Later on it gave generously to many educational projects. The other society began in 1701, and was called the Society for the Propagation of the Gospel in Foreign Parts (S.P.G.). Although it was originally intended to help colonists, it shortly decided to make every effort to convert heathen and infidels. These two great Societies have flourished to the present day, and reference will be made continually to their work in these pages. The founder of both Societies was the Reverend Dr. Thomas Bray, the Bishop of London's famous Commissary to the American colonies.

The American Revolution was a great victory for the colonists and a dismal defeat for England; but great good came out of it for Anglicanism, for when the political autonomy of the United States was established, the ecclesiastical autonomy of the Colonial Church was likewise guaranteed. The United Church of England and Ireland now had an independent daughter and the Anglican Communion had come into being. Within a few years the new Church had obtained its first bishop, and not from England but from Scotland. It was a salutary shock for the English Church to discover that if they would not supply episcopal orders for clergymen who owed no allegiance to England, there were other bishops who could and would. In a very short time after Samuel Seabury's consecration the necessary parliamentary legislation for this was passed, and in 1787 two more bishops were consecrated for the United States and one for Canada by the English Archbishops and Bishops.

The end of the eighteenth century witnessed the founding of a third missionary agency, the Church Missionary Society

(C.M.S.). The sixteen clergy and nine laymen who met at the "Castle and Falcon" in Aldersgate Street, near the place where Wesley felt his heart "strangely warmed," were all evangelical members of the Church of England; the Reverend John Venn was the chairman. Like its precursors, S.P.G. and S.P.C.K., C.M.S. is still at work, and has written many stirring pages in the missionary story of the Anglican Communion.

From the turn of the century onwards the missionary vision of the Church developed rapidly. The effects of the Evangelical Revival were a heightened sense of duty to carry the Gospel to the farthest corners of the earth, while the later Oxford Movement gave to Englishmen a new sense of their Catholic heritage and their duty to share it as widely as possible.

In 1814 a bishop had been appointed to Calcutta; he was the first of an ever-increasing number of apostolic missionaries to be consecrated for overseas. These latter were mostly men of sterling worth who gave Englishmen a new and welcome idea of what a bishop could be; also they were God's agents in establishing Anglicanism among people of many races and nationalities beyond the English-speaking world.

The bishops of those days were issued Letters Patent by the government before their consecration. This was a grant of authority, in the form of a Royal Mandate, to persons appointed to be bishops, and it defined the area of jurisdiction. But the system soon broke down when colonies were given self-government.

Some idea of the growth of the Anglican Communion overseas may be gathered from the fact that while in the year 1840 there were only ten dioceses outside the British Isles, the number had increased to forty-one by the year 1861.

Bishop Alfred Barry recalls an epochal day in 1847 when four colonial bishops were consecrated at a great service in Westminster Abbey, one for Capetown and three for Australia.[7] The very fact that such a service was held in the Abbey indicates the upsurge of interest in missionary matters by members of the Church of England. It was in notable contrast to the almost secret consecrations of Middleton and Heber for India, just a few years before, at Lambeth Palace Chapel.

The Statesman-Bishop of London, Charles James Blomfield, deserves much credit for underwriting the colonial missionary expansion of those days, for in 1841 he founded the "Colonial Bishoprics Fund" for the endowment of new missionary dioceses. The Fund received almost one million pounds for this purpose from the time of its foundation to the turn of the century, and it was instrumental in providing endowments for the bishops' salaries in sixty-seven new colonial dioceses. The famous Baroness Angela Burdett-Coutts endowed three bishoprics and well deserved the reward of being buried in Westminster Abbey.

This phenomenal growth brought with it perplexing problems, which could now be debated in the open, Convocation having been restored in 1852. Times had changed, for until the middle of the nineteenth century the Anglican Church had been held together by "Letters Patent, the oath of obedience to Canterbury, crown appointments, a common episcopate, and common standards of faith and worship."[8] The Episcopal Church in the United States of America was already independent, and colonial dioceses became more and more independent through synods which they themselves called. Actually, the calling of a synod anywhere in the Anglican Church was illegal according to an Act of

Henry VIII which made it clear that synods could be called only with the royal consent!

The various self-governing branches of what was now a worldwide Church felt an increasing need for common counsel, and although the idea had been talked about for some time, it was the Canadian Church which officially asked the Archbishop of Canterbury in 1864 if he could suggest some way "by which the members of our Anglican Communion in all quarters of the world should have a share in the deliberations for her welfare and be permitted to have a representation in one General Council of her members gathered from every land." [9]

Archbishop Longley weighed the matter carefully and, in due course, sent out one hundred forty-four invitations to Anglican bishops all over the world to attend a conference in 1867 at Lambeth Palace, his London residence. Seventy-six bishops accepted, and since that time, seven more Lambeth Conferences have been held. The dates, together with the number of bishops attending make interesting reading: 1867—72; 1878—100; 1888—145; 1897—194; 1908—242; 1920—252; 1930—307; 1948—329. The first conference was much concerned with the authority of bishops and metropolitans in their respective Provinces, but the subject matter widened quickly, for by 1878 the unity of the Anglican Church was discussed at length. Christian reunion, Christian witness, Faith and Doctrine, missionary strategy, and moral, social, ethical, and political problems have all had their place on the programs of the several conferences. The Conference is a conference, and in no sense is it a legislative body, although the Encyclical Letter which it promulgates after each session has great moral authority.

In 1954 an Anglican Congress was held in Minneapolis, Minnesota, to which came 201 bishops, 242 priests, and 214 lay persons from all over the world. The Congress did much to give to every branch of the Church a new sense of oneness, a new sense of thankfulness for the riches of their common heritage, and a new missionary zeal. It is contemplated that a similar Congress be held every decade between meetings of the Lambeth Conference.

The Anglican Church is at once Catholic and Protestant; it is a living demonstration that two apparently antithetical approaches to the Christian faith can be synthesized in a vital and enduring fellowship. Anglicans are Catholics because they believe in the Catholic Scriptures, in the Catholic creeds, in the Catholic sacraments of Baptism and Holy Communion, and in the Catholic threefold order of the Ministry. Anglicans are Protestants because they reject papal claims as false to history and to the true faith, and because they insist that the Faith be rooted and grounded in the Holy Scriptures. The very presence of the Anglican Church in the world today is a salutary witness that it is possible to hold the true Catholic faith without submitting to a highly centralized and wholly authoritarian ecclesiastical system. This is of the greatest importance to the cause of freedom now and in the future, for no absolutist church can ever be content, in the long run, to live with a free democracy.

The Anglican Church is spread over a large part of the world, and its three hundred and thirty-one dioceses comprise a baptized membership of at least 34,000,000. The studied aim of the Anglican Church is the creation of a growing number of self-governing provinces or national churches, each under national leadership and each in communion with

23

the See of Canterbury. Two such Provinces, West Africa and Central Africa, have been inaugurated in the last six years, and more will doubtless follow in the future.]

THE CHURCH IN WALES

Writing in A.D. 210, Tertullian declared that "there are places of the Britons unapproached by the Romans but subdued to Christ." Perhaps he was referring to that western part of the Island now known as Wales, where the Christian faith had arrived some years before. The Church in Wales was separate from the Church in England, and it remained so until the twelfth century when it became part of the province of Canterbury and subject to the Archbishop and Crown. This relationship continued until the twentieth century when the Church in Wales again became autonomous.

It is likely that the Christian Faith had spread over most of what is now England and Wales by the beginning of the fifth century, when the land enjoyed a measure of peace. This peace came to an end with the departure of the Roman legions. Many Britons from the eastern areas were pushed westward under the pressure of Saxon attacks, and ended up in Wales. In spite of upheavals this age proved to be a great one for Christianity, and has been called "the golden age of Welsh saints," for great men like Gildas, Dewi (David), Asaph, Garmon, and Deiniol flourished.

The representatives of the Welsh Church with whom Augustine of Canterbury met at Down Amprey in 603 were Celtic bishops who had refused to recognize the Italian missionary as their superior since, as they told him, they did not owe him any obedience. Indeed, the Welsh Church was slow to reach agreements with the Church in Britain, and it only accepted the Latin date for keeping Easter in 768. Even then the Welsh Church had no thought of submitting to Canterbury. Welsh patriots fought to keep their Church free of both the English throne and the Pope. In the twelfth century, however, the Welsh Church finally submitted to Canterbury.

The Reformation caused much dislocation in Wales, although there was not too much active opposition to it. One difficulty, that of language, could have been obviated had the Crown realized that few Welshmen wanted to speak or read English. With an incredible lack of understanding the Welsh Church was ordered in 1549 to hold its services in English, which was much more of a foreign tongue to most Welshmen than the familiar Latin. However, in 1551 William Salesbury made a Welsh translation of the Epistles and Gospels for Sundays and Saints' Days; and in 1566 Bishop Richard Davies of St. David's translated the Prayer Book into Welsh. The following year he and Salesbury translated the whole of the New Testament. By 1588 the translation of the whole Bible into Welsh was completed—the work of the great Bishop William Morgan of St. Asaph, who not only did the translating but who also superintended the printing of the Bible.

This was all to the good and the Church would undoubtedly have gone forward had it been left alone, but it had hardly recovered from the Reformation before the reign of Cromwell and his Puritans wrought great havoc throughout the land. One could ride twenty miles in Wales in those days without finding a resident minister, and ignorant manual laborers were put in charge of parishes whose clergy had supported Charles I. For the fourteen years between 1646 and 1660 not a single Anglican ordination took place, and the sacraments were seldom administered. To their credit, it must be said that the Puritans did a great deal for the education of the people, but they used confiscated Church funds to finance their plans.

The weakness of the Welsh Church in the eighteenth century was in great measure due to the events of the Reformation and the Commonwealth, and it was not until well along in that century that the visitation returns of the bishops show an uptrend. A further problem arose because the British government was accustomed to manipulate Welsh bishoprics for political purposes, as testing places for men they wished to use as tools.

Fortunately, there came a reaction against the secularism of the times which took the form of a great evangelistic revival, led by one Griffith Jones, a priest and the vicar of Llanddowrer. S.P.C.K. had instituted schools in Wales and had supplied teachers for them some years before, so Jones built on the foundation and developed it until he had Circulating Schools all over Wales. Among other things the pupils were taught to read the Welsh Bible. It was so successful a venture that by the year of Jones's death in 1761, it is estimated that he had reached more than 150,000 people. These schools laid the groundwork for the preaching evangelists, Whitefield and John Wesley, who conducted revivals in Wales beginning about 1740. All three men, Jones, Whitefield, and Wesley were Anglican priests, so it can be said with truth that the leaders of the new movement were Churchmen. It was not until 1810 that the Methodists broke away, a tragedy that lost most of the middle and laboring classes to the Church.

The growth of dissent in the nineteenth century brought on the movement to disestablish the Welsh Church. The agitation that commenced in 1832 became quite strong by 1870, when a bill for disestablishment was introduced in Parliament. The proponents of the bill claimed that the Welsh Church was not fulfilling its task and that it represented but a small proportion of the population. Gladstone strongly opposed the bill on the several occasions in his lifetime that it was introduced. In 1914, however, the bill passed as the "Welsh Church Act." The real issue proved to be not the establishment but the Church endowments which amounted to 268,550 pounds a year. All but 90,357 pounds, the income of endowments left the Church since 1662, was confiscated and given to the University of Wales and the County Councils. The Act was not put into effect until 1920, due to the First World War; but on the Feast of the Epiphany of that year the Archbishop of Canterbury created a new and autonomous province of the Anglican Communion. The Bishop of St. Asaph was elected as the first Archbishop, and he was enthroned at St. Asaph by Archbishop Davidson on June 1, 1920. The new Province had four dioceses at first, but Monmouth was set apart in 1921 and Swansea and Brecon two years later, making the present total of six dioceses.

Under the Constitution the Governing Body is the supreme legislative arm of the Church, consisting of the Archbishop and Bishops, some five hundred clergy and laity, and certain other elected and co-opted members. There is also a Representative Body of about one hundred members, which holds and administers the Church property, pays grants and stipends, and attends to the general financing of the Church and its work. The Representative Body is subject to the control of the Governing Body, but it is given rather wide discretionary powers.

The diocesan bishops are chosen by an electoral college

which consists of the House of Bishops, three clergy and three laymen elected from each of six dioceses, and six clergy and six laymen elected from the diocese in which the vacancy exists. In the event that the college fails to elect by a two-thirds vote, the nomination goes to the Archbishop of Canterbury. Any diocesan bishop is eligible for election to the archbishopric.

In spite of the tremendous setback caused by disendowment, the Church in Wales shows many signs of new vigor. The Education Act of 1944 came about largely because of the advocacy of the Welsh Church, with the result that the teaching of religion has been restored to the public schools, and local educational authorities know they are responsible for religious and moral teaching as well as for the secular disciplines.

There are two independent church colleges where ordinands are trained, as well as church-operated hostels for men at the Universities of Bangor and Cardiff. There is also a theological college at Llandaff, while Lampeter has a theological department.

The Church is the largest religious body in Wales having a baptized membership of some 600,000, and there are indications that Noncomformity is on the decline, with a consequent renewal of interest in the ancient Church in Wales. At the time of its disestablishment the Welsh Church agreed to use the Church of England Prayer Book of 1662 until such time as a revision was desired. Soon after World War II, the Church set about Prayer Book revision, beginning with the Occasional Offices, the Lectionary, and the Kalendar. It is expected that the total revision will not be completed for some years to come.

THE EPISCOPAL CHURCH
IN SCOTLAND

The Venerable Bede tells us that Pope Siricius sent a Scots youth named Ninian to evangelize his fellowcountry-men in 394, and that when the latter returned home to southern Scotland, many Christians welcomed him there. At any rate, the monastery that Ninian founded spread its influence to Ireland, from whence St. Columba came in the sixth century to preach the Gospel in Scotland. The latter founded the great monastery of Iona, and the influence of this establishment spread far and wide, for by the time of St. Columba's death in 597 there were Christian settlements as far north as Aberdeen and Banff. The Church at this period followed the pattern of the British Church in the days before Augustine. These early bishops probably followed the Celtic fashion of having tribal jurisdiction, and it fell to the noble Queen Margaret, daughter of Edward the Confessor and wife of King Malcolm of Scotland, to introduce the diocesan system in the eleventh century. She did much to strengthen the Church and, among other pious deeds, built the famous church and abbey of Dunfermline.

The eleventh century witnessed a continuation of the fusion between Celtic and Roman Christianity, and the old system where monastic abbots ruled the Church gave way to distinct dioceses, each under the rule of a bishop. Towards the end of the twelfth century, eleven such dioceses had been formed in the south. The people in the north were still under the control of Norway, and the Christians in that area owed allegiance to the metropolitan of Drontheim.

Papal influence increased steadily in the twelfth century

29

and it was possible for the Pope to put the whole of Scotland under an interdict in 1178 because of a disputed episcopal election, while another interdict in 1217 lasted a whole year. Not that papal power was unchallenged, for in 1442 when the Pope made the See of St. Andrew's an archbishopric, vigorous protests came from the Archbishop of York, the Metropolitan of Drontheim, and the Scottish bishops, on the grounds that the action had been taken without consultation with them and without their consent.

The widespread degeneracy of the Church in Europe was apparent also in Scotland where the open sale of Church offices to the highest bidder, the corruption of many clergy and a general laxity in religious matters gave the ambitious nobility a sufficient reason to make common cause against both the Church and the Crown. Lutheranism spread to Scotland and its first exponent, one Patrick Hamilton, was burned at the stake, the first of many to suffer for their religious convictions in Scotland over the next two centuries. Cardinal Beaton was murdered in 1546, and by 1560 the Reformed Church under John Knox and the "Lords of the Congregation" was set up in Scotland as the national faith. It was a complete break with the medieval Church, and established on the model of Calvin's Geneva: there was, for instance, no laying on of hands at ordinations from 1560 to 1580. The title of "bishop" was kept as were the old diocesan boundaries, but the bishops were really superintendents without either the functions or the authority of bishops as the ancient Church understood the same. Episcopacy was really abolished together with the liturgy and the observance of Church festivals.

It was at this troublous time that Mary Queen of Scots landed at Leith in 1561 to take up the Crown that had been hers for almost two decades. She was received with great enthusiasm at first, but the fact that she was a Roman Catholic and that she set out to make herself an absolute monarch determined John Knox and his followers to end her reign. Mary was forced to abdicate in favor of her son James in 1567, and the country came under a regency until 1581 when James VI began to rule in his own right. The years 1575-1590 witnessed a bitter struggle between the Presbyterian and the Episcopal parties within the Church, until by the latter year two distinct churches emerged. James VI of Scotland had become James I of England in 1603, and seven years later he called together a General Assembly at Glasgow where it was agreed that three bishops were to be consecrated for Scotland in England and so restore the normal succession. This was done; and although the Scottish Church had no liturgy, it might have grown into some semblance of orthodoxy except for Charles I, who succeeded his father in 1625. Charles ordered the Scottish nobles to restore the property they had taken from the Church, but many of the great landowners had become Protestants to get church property and had become Covenanters in order to keep it.

Charles issued Canons and a constitution for the Church of Scotland similar to those of the Church of England, and he followed this by an attempt to force the Book of Common Prayer on the unwilling Scots. Feelings ran high and violent rioting ensued, and it is recorded that upon one occasion the Bishop of Brechin felt obliged to read the new Liturgy with a brace of loaded pistols lying before him on the reading desk! More than pistols were needed, as Charles discovered, when the Scottish General Assembly met in 1638, deposed all bishops, restored Presbyterianism and set up a second reformation. Charles took to the field but his forces were defeated by the significant combination of English Puritans and Scottish Calvinists.

The Restoration of 1660, which followed Cromwell's years of the Protectorate, saw another reversal in policy for the Scottish Church, for in 1661 four bishops were consecrated for Scotland in Westminster Abbey, among them James Sharp as Archbishop of Saint Andrews. In spite of the fact that these bishops consecrated nine more men to the episcopate, each with a diocesan jurisdiction, and that many Presbyterian clergy submitted to episcopal ordination under the new law, the restored Church was more Calvinist then Anglican. It had no liturgy, it was tied to the English Crown, and its services were not very different from the drab Presbyterian ritual.

The Presbyterian element finally triumphed, for open rebellion started in the year of Charles II's death in 1685, when Archbishop Sharp was murdered. James II reigned only three years before he fled, but his attempted policy of religious toleration was suspected because of his open espousal of Roman Catholicism. Also, it was too late because the Calvinist element in the Church of Scotland wanted not compromise but victory. The new King William of Orange gave the Presbyterians his support, so once more episcopacy was abolished even though two thirds of the population were Episcopalians. Most of these latter were fatally enamoured of the Stuarts, while their bishops would not take an oath of loyalty to any other king as long as a Stuart monarch lived to whom they had pledged their loyalty. Since "Bonnie Prince Charlie" did not die until 1788, the situation of the Episcopalians, now a separate Church, went from bad to worse.

William made overtures to the bishops early in his reign, asking them to accept the Royal Supremacy, and the British

32

Parliament passed an Act of Toleration for Scottish Episcopalians in 1712. However, the bishops ("non-jurors") steadfastly refused the proffered olive branch, but some laypeople accepted the government's offer and were allowed to have public worship; they used the English Book of Common Prayer, got their clergy from England and were thus the origin of the "qualified" congregations as they were called. As the years went on, and as the cause of the non-jurors became increasingly hopeless, these congregations grew in strength and ultimately contributed largely to the revival of the Church in Scotland.

For the most part, however, the Episcopalians were staunch supporters of the Stuart or Jacobite cause and many of them took part in the rebellions of 1715 and 1745 under the Old and the Young Pretender. This brought more persecution, particularly unhappy because it was now quite evident that the Stuart cause was hopeless. Whatever their personal qualities it is difficult not to agree that Dr. Johnson was justified in his remark, 'I never knew a non-juror who could reason'. [10] The fatal fanaticism of the non-jurors for the faithless Stuarts almost killed the Church.

Be that as it may, it was the feeble Scottish Church that gave the first bishop to the American Church, for Samuel Seabury came to Scotland for consecration after having failed to secure apostolic orders at the hands of the English bishops. Since the Scottish Church was disestablished, it had no worries about its relationship to the Crown. While its bishops were valid and proper bishops, they had no official government status, and therefore no official entanglements. It was on November 14, 1784, that Seabury was consecrated for Connecticut in the private chapel of Bishop John Skinner at Aberdeen by Bishops Kilgour, Petrie, and Skinner. At this time there were but four bishops and forty clergy in the whole of Scotland.

Four years later Prince Charles Edward, the young Pretender died, and at long last the Scottish bishops formally recognized the House of Hanover with the result that the penal laws were gradually repealed. Bishop John Skinner, one of Seabury's consecrators, is the great figure of this period. As an ecclesiastical statesman, he occupied in the Scottish Church a position similar to that of White in the American Church. Skinner worked successfully to secure the repeal of the penal laws; he shepherded many congregations of "qualified chapels" into the Church; he persuaded a Convocation of Clergy in 1804 to accept the Thirty-nine Articles; and he called the First General Synod in 1811 of bishops, deans, and clergy for drawing up canons for the governance of the Church. Skinner died in 1816 and was succeeded in the See of Aberdeen by his son William (1816-1857), so that for over seventy years the Church had the benefit of a brilliant father and an able son.

The times were changing, for when George IV visited Scotland in 1820, he received in audience the six Scottish bishops who assured the King of their own loyalty and of the loyalty of their Church to the Crown. Had this happened a century earlier the story of the Scottish Church might well have been vastly different. The Church now began a period of growth from about 1840 to the end of the century, a growth that was helped by notable leadership, the Oxford Movement, and the establishment in 1840 of Glenalmond College for educating both clergy and laity. In the two decades 1838-58 the number of churches grew from seventy-three to one hundred fifty and the clergy from seventy-eight to one hundred sixty-three.

The three elements in the Church likewise began to grow together in this period. These elements were the old non-juring congregations who were quite orthodox and mostly in the North; the "qualified chapels" whose adherents were often of English or Irish birth and who used the Church of England Prayer Book; and Anglo-Catholics from England.

The laity became more prominent in the life of the Church during the nineteenth century, for lay participation in church government was advocated by the American Bishop John Henry Hobart when he visited Scotland in 1824. William Ewart Gladstone was also its firm advocate. It is interesting to observe that laymen took part in episcopal elections from 1863 onwards. A representative Church Council instituted by the Provincial Synod in 1876 was a great forward step in the Church's life, and it remains the recognized organ in financial matters. It is made up of bishops, deans, clergy, diocesan officials and laymen from every parish and mission.

The new vigor of the Church was expressed also in new buildings, for towards the end of the nineteenth century cathedrals were built at Inverness, Edinburgh, and Perth. The latter, begun in 1850, was the first cathedral to be built in Britain since the new St. Paul's had been erected after the Great Fire of London of 1666.

Interest in overseas mission work came comparatively late, but in 1871 the Church supplied a bishop for St. John's, Kaffraria, and shortly afterwards it began work in Chanda, India. It is a matter of interest that the Scottish Church has sent out bishops for Tasmania, Gibraltar, Western Europe, and Madagascar, and, in recent years, an Archbishop of Capetown.

The Scottish Book of Common Prayer, revised in 1929, is now in general use throughout the Church, although the

Church of England Prayer Book may also be used. Each of the seven dioceses has its bishop and diocesan synod, while the Provincial Synod is presided over by the elected Primus who is not a Metropolitan. The membership of the Church rose sharply from 1840 onwards, reaching 60,000 by 1870, 116,000 by the turn of the century, and 147,000 in 1921.

THE CHURCH OF IRELAND

The Christian faith must have been introduced in Ireland some time in the third century, for by the middle of the next century we hear of a notable Christian named Kieran; and there are several other indications that Christian missionaries lived in the southwest part of the Island at that time.

St. Patrick is, of course, the great Apostle of the Irish as well as the patron saint of the land. Born in Dumbarton, Scotland, about 372, he was sold as a slave to an Irish chieftain when he was but sixteen. After six years Patrick escaped to Gaul, and after some years of travel and study he was consecrated a bishop and returned to Ireland about 403. He established the See of Armagh, and until his death more than sixty years later, he devoted himself to the conversion of his fellow-countrymen and to the upbuilding of the Church there.

The Church in Ireland in those days followed the Celtic tradition and it was definitely centered around monasteries which were governed by abbots. While bishops ordained men, they had no fixed dioceses and there were no parishes. For all this seeming lack of organization, the period from the sixth to the eighth centuries was a time of tremendous missionary activity on the part of the Irish Church. Their missionaries took the Gospel to Britain and they were key figures in the conversion of northern Europe. St. Columba left Ireland in 563 and founded Iona as a missionary base for the conversion of northern Britain. St. Columbanus left Ireland for Gaul about 590 and, in the teeth of great opposition, he established monasteries there. One of his followers, St. Gall, was largely responsible for Christianizing parts of what are now Switzerland and Baden.

Ireland escaped invasion until the coming of the Danes and Vikings, but these roving Norsemen kept the land in an almost continuous turmoil for some two hundred years. The invasions were the more effective because there was no king over all the land—only petty chieftains who quarrelled with one another and connived with the invaders. The Church was well-nigh wrecked and some of her ablest men fled, among them John Scotus Erigena. The opening of the eleventh century saw Brian Boru, King of Munster, break the power of the invaders and become undisputed overlord until his death in 1014. By the time of the Conquest many of the Norsemen had become Christian and they soon asked for bishops, not from the Irish, but from their Norman cousins now ruling in England. Until this time the Irish kept their own form of Christianity, but in 1072 Lanfranc, Archbishop of Canterbury, claimed jurisdiction over this island to the west.

In 1118, there was held a great synod at Rathbreasil, presided over by a papal legate for the first time in Irish Church history, and the land was organized into four ecclesiastical provinces and twenty-five dioceses after the Roman pattern. The Roman liturgy took the place of the Celtic use, church endowments were transferred to the diocesan bishops, and missionaries from the Continent founded monasteries. By 1148, at the Synod of Kells, the number of dioceses was increased to thirty-four, with four archbishops instead of two, and strict laws were made against the marriage of clergy. Until this time clerical marriages had been quite customary, and indeed they took place as late as the fifteenth century. St. Patrick himself was the grandson of a priest.

Henry II of England was granted the overlordship of Ireland by the Pope in 1155, and although he took possession of the land he never conquered it. There was, however, a determined effort to make the Irish Church follow the English pattern, and many English ecclesiastics were given high office in the Irish Church. England's wars on the Continent and her internal strife helped the Irish to gain back much of the land from which they had been dispossessed by the English, so that by 1366 the sphere of English rule had been reduced to a small area around Dublin called the "Pale." It was a time of great distress for the Irish Church when monasteries in the control of "foreigners" enjoyed comparative wealth, while the Irish clergy remained miserably poor.

Ireland was untouched by the revival of learning in Europe, for she had no university during the Renaissance or the Reformation. The first printing press was not set up until about 1550, and the first foundation of learning was Trinity College, in Dublin, founded in 1591 by Queen Elizabeth.

The Church of Ireland came under the complete control of England in 1536, and the anti-papal legislation of Henry VIII was reiterated in Ireland. A plot in 1539 between some Irish chieftains and Francis I of France, which had been instigated by the Pope, failed to overthrow the English power, with the result that the majority of the Irish leaders accepted the Royal Supremacy.

The great weakness of the Reformation in Ireland lay in

the fact that most of the people lived in the country and spoke no English. No attempt was made to preach the Gospel in the native tongue or to translate the Bible and the Book of Common Prayer into Gaelic until it was too late. Neither the Gaelic New Testament nor the Holy Communion service were available until 1603, and the Book of Common Prayer in the Gaelic tongue was not forthcoming until five years later.

Elizabeth was forced to keep control of Ireland to prevent Spanish plots, but the control was accompanied by much bloodshed, confiscation of land, and the settlement of English colonists. The Reformation was thus inevitably associated in Irish minds with foreign rule, and this precluded its widespread acceptance by the people.

The apostolic succession of bishops was kept intact throughout the Reformation period, and Adam Loftus was properly consecrated for Armagh in 1563. However, the Pope had appointed a rival Archbishop of Armagh two years earlier, and increasing numbers of papal missionaries, as agents of the Counter-Reformation, won many Irish back to the Roman fold. Conditions in the parishes were very bad, for in Meath in the year 1556 it was reported that 105 out of 224 churches were without settled clergy.

During the reign of Charles I the Earl of Strafford became Viceroy of Ireland and he managed to bring some order out of the chaos. Real progress was made until the coming of the Civil War in England and the following invasion of Ireland by Oliver Cromwell in 1649 with its savagery and massacre. Eight bishops survived those perilous days and twelve more were consecrated in 1661; so the Church had good leadership at last. Archbishop Bramhall belongs to this period, and it was he who caused the Bible to be translated into Gaelic. Another notable figure was Jeremy Taylor, the Bishop of Down and Connor—a Churchman who would have been reckoned great in any age.

The short reign of James II stirred up more trouble, for he deliberately left Irish bishoprics vacant in order to give their revenues to the Roman Catholic bishops. William of Orange, King of England, defeated James at the Battle of the Boyne, and from then onwards the Irish parliament came increasingly under the control of England, and Irish bishoprics became the political appointments of the English Ministry. In spite of these real problems, the Church produced at least two notable men in the early eighteenth century: the satirist, Jonathan Swift, who became Dean of St. Patrick's Cathedral in Dublin in 1713; and George Berkeley, world-renowned philosopher, who was appointed to the deanery of Derry in 1724, and became Bishop of Cloyne a decade later. The Toleration Act had become law in 1719, but the following decades witnessed a growing spirit of indifference to religion, while large emigration from the North of Ireland to Nova Scotia and the West Indies further weakened the Irish Church.

The Irish Act of Union in 1800 brought about the political union of Ireland and Great Britain, and it also brought into being the "United Church of England and Ireland." This is the nucleus of the Anglican Communion. The United Church soon felt the antagonistic weight of the British Parliament which suppressed ten out of the twenty-two Irish bishoprics and reduced the archbishoprics from four to two by the "Church Temporalities Act." This action was taken without consultation with the Irish bishops. Nevertheless, the Church was growing in this period, for in 1840 it numbered some 800,000 out of a total population of eight million.

40

It is a proportion that has not changed much to the present day with the population reduced to one-half of what it was a century ago.

Parliament disestablished and disendowed the Irish Church by an Act of 1869, an event which the Church prepared for by the calling of a General Synod in 1870 for the purpose of setting up its own government. The Synod erected a Constitution and made provision for two Houses, the House of Bishops and the House of Clergy and Laymen which was to meet as one House. The procedure envisioned was parliamentary rather then synodical, with proposed canons receiving first, second, and third hearings. A unique feature of the Irish Church is the provision for twice as many laymen as clergy for General Synod, an indication of an anti-clerical attitude which had long been a feature of the Church's life. General Synod must meet for a week every year. A representative body of elected, co-opted, and ex-officio members acts as a corporation for holding trust funds and for raising various monies.

Diocesan synods were also set up, and here again there are twice as many lay representatives as there are clergy, the laity having an equal voice in all questions that come before the synod. The Archbishop of Armagh is elected by the House of Bishops from among their number. There are two provinces, Armagh and Dublin, each with an Archbishop.

The Church of Ireland met the challenge of disestablishment and the more serious blow of disendowment with courage and fortitude, and in the long run the effects have been wholesome. The Church has taken its place as an autonomous and fully self-governing member of the Anglican Communion. At its initial Synod in 1870 the Church expressed clearly that its faith was the faith of the Anglican

Church, and that it could not be in communion with any Church that was not fully episcopal.

The agitation for Home Rule for Ireland grew in strength towards the end of the nineteenth century, but the Church of Ireland opposed the bills introduced into Parliament for this purpose in 1886 and 1893. The First World War and the Easter Rebellion of 1916 were followed by the passing of the Home Rule Bill in 1920. Since very few members of the Church of Ireland took up the cause of freedom, the result has been that its political and social influence declined during those troubled years.

The Irish Book of Common Prayer differs very little from the English Book. The revision of 1878 strikes a puritan note in some of its rubrics as it indicates also the influence of members with a strong presbyterian background. The north end of the Holy Table is the only legal position for saying the Prayer of Consecration at the Holy Communion, no candles or cross are allowed on the Table, and eucharistic vestments are forbidden. A new revision after World War I succeeded remarkably in enriching the Prayer Book without entering into questions of doctrine; it was begun in 1909 and completed in 1926.

The Church is much stronger in Northern Ireland where it numbers 353,000 or some thirty per cent of the population; and this part of the Church is steadily increasing in strength. In Eire it is very much a minority group with something less than five per cent of the people on its rolls.

The Church has no missionary society of its own, but it has had a college mission from Trinity, Dublin, working in China and India. Also, the Church in Ireland has had some responsibility for the Reformed Episcopal Church in Spain and Portugal, and has consecrated several bishops for that

Church. The most recent was the consecration of the Right Reverend Santos Molina at Madrid, Spain, on April 29, 1956, by the Right Reverend James McCann of the Church of Ireland with the Right Reverend Stephen E. Keeler, the late Bishop of Minnesota, and the Right Reverend Reginald Mallett of Northern Indiana, as co-consecrators.

Most of the clergy are trained in the Divinity School at Trinity College, where the scholarship is high, but where the students do not get the obvious advantage of attending a regular theological college.

CHAPTER TWO

The Americas
and the West Indies

The Americas
and the West Indies

THE PROTESTANT EPISCOPAL CHURCH
IN THE UNITED STATES OF AMERICA

The expansion of Europe which has been called the "most colossal cultural change that has ever taken place in the history of mankind" was triggered by Columbus' voyage, which was followed by intrepid adventurers of many European nations. Among them was Sir Francis Drake who went westward in 1577 at his sovereign's command to "annoy the King of Spain in his Indies," in the process of which he landed near San Francisco on June 24, 1579. The Reverend Francis Fletcher, chaplain of the *Golden Hind*, held a Prayer Book service on shore, and Drake claimed the land for Good Queen Bess calling it Nova Albion. The original claimplate discovered in recent years is now in the possession of the California Historical Society. Also there is a "Prayer Book Cross" in Golden Gate Park, marking the approximate site of this first Prayer Book Service in what is now the United States.

The story of the Episcopal Church really begins with the landing of a colony in Jamestown, Virginia, when their chaplain, Robert Hunt, celebrated the Holy Communion

47

under "an olde sail" on May 14, 1607. This is the first recorded celebration of the Holy Communion in what is now the United States. It took place thirteen years before the landing of the Mayflower Pilgrims. After many initial difficulties, the colony began to flourish, and twelve years after its founding a legislature was provided for in Virginia and provision made for the support of the Church.

The Mayflower Pilgrims who landed at Plymouth Rock in Massachusetts in 1620 had already separated themselves from the Church of England, and had set up a theocracy in the Massachusetts Bay area along with the Puritans who had later settled in and around Boston. They became increasingly restive and antagonistic to the Church of England and even when King's Chapel was organized by Anglicans in 1686, it took all the authority of the Royal Governor, Andros, to see that a site was secured for the church building. The continued and considerable opposition of the Independents towards the Church of England caused a number of thoughtful people to become Anglicans; among them was Timothy Cutler, a former president of Yale, who became the first rector of Christ Church, Boston, in 1723. When Cutler died, after a ministry there of forty-two years, his congregation numbered some eight hundred persons.

In New York, the chapel in the old Dutch fort of New Amsterdam became the scene of Prayer Book services when the Dutch colony was surrendered to the British in 1664. Not long afterwards, Trinity Church on Lower Manhattan was organized by leading Anglicans and called its first incumbent, William Vesey, in 1697. A half century later Anglicans were largely instrumental in founding King's College, now Columbia University. Philadelphia did not get its first Anglican church until 1694 with the organization of

48

Christ Church in that city. It is interesting to note that the Anglican Church was fully established in Virginia, and partly established in New York State, South Carolina, North Carolina, and Georgia.

The Bishop of London had the ecclesiastical oversight of the Colonies, and in spite of the obvious difficulties of such an arrangement, a number of the bishops of that see during colonial days took their overseas obligation seriously, and sent commissaries to the Colonies. It was Bishop Henry Compton of London, who sent the great Thomas Bray as his Commissary, or bishop's representative, to Maryland in 1699. Bray made a series of visitations and returned to England, where he so ably presented the needs and opportunities of the Church in the Colonies that he was able to obtain a Royal Charter for the incorporation of the "Society for the Propagation of the Gospel in Foreign Parts" in 1701. There were some sixty Anglican clergy in the Colonies by 1700, forty of whom were in Virginia and Maryland. From that time until the Revolution, the Society sent three hundred and thirty-eight missionaries to America, although some were shipwrecked on the way and never saw their overseas parishes. The Society likewise poured out money in considerable amounts for libraries and other equipment for missionary work amongst the Colonists, the Negroes, and the Indians.

The Anglicans were at a tremendous disadvantage compared to the Independents, for the latter had no bishops and could therefore ordain their own men on the spot, whereas any colonist who sought Anglican ordination had to travel six thousand miles to England and back. Furthermore, while the Anglican system depended on bishops to ordain, to confirm, and to govern, the Church remained throughout the colonial period an episcopal Church without an episcopate.

The Independents in the Colonies fought any attempt to bring a bishop to America, for they knew nothing of a bishop who was neither a political officer nor an agent of the King of England. Since Convocation had been suppressed in England in 1717, the Church had no corporate and effective voice to make its needs known, and the government would do nothing to issue Letters Patent for an American bishop for fear of offending the already sensitive Congregationalists in the Colonies.

Many attempts were made to provide a bishop for America from 1633 onwards, and S.P.G. did its best to move both Crown and Parliament to act. Two memorials to Queen Anne for this purpose had good chance of success but for Her Majesty's untimely death at the age of forty-nine. Bishop Sherlock of London, and others, drew up a workable plan in 1750 which, among other items, provided for a colonial bishop who would be devoid of political and governmental authority, but by this time the great divisive forces were at work and the plan was given up. A bitter pamphlet warfare from 1768 onwards turned the question of a colonial bishop into a political issue, and it became a real factor in the growing alienation of the Colonists from England.

The consequences of the Revolution to the colonial Anglican Church were nothing short of disastrous. The enmity and cruel persecution of Anglicans by the Independents during the war; the fact that many Anglican clergy and not a few laity were outspoken Loyalists; the mass migrations of many thousands of Anglicans to Canada; the confiscation of endowments and glebe lands by the states; and the absence of episcopal authority—all combined to make the Church's future appear hopeless indeed. In addition, the S.P.G. cut off all its support to the clergy and parishes. Not that all the

Anglicans were Loyalists by any means, for George Washington was only one of many outstanding colonists who sided with the revolutionaries, and it is well known that thirty-five of the fifty-six signers of the Declaration of Independence were Anglicans.

The Church was now on her own resources, the first of the British colonial churches to achieve this status. It had need of bishops to ordain and confirm, a Constitution by which it could govern itself, and a modified Book of Common Prayer with which it could worship. These three needs were satisfied in a surprisingly short space of time.

William White, rector of Christ Church, Philadelphia, published a pamphlet wherein he advised that the Church temporarily adopt a presbyterian system of government since bishops "could not be had." This caused alarm in Connecticut with the result that ten of the fourteen clergy of the forty congregations met in Convention at the Glebe House in Woodbury, Connecticut, March 25, 1783, and elected Samuel Seabury as their bishop, giving him instructions to proceed at once to England to seek consecration at the hands of the Archbishops of England. The astute New Englanders, who knew of previous failures to obtain an episcopate before the war, further instructed their bishop-elect to seek apostolic orders from the Scottish bishops should he fail in his mission in England. Seabury did not get these latter instructions but he went to Scotland eventually on his own initiative, for he had worshipped with the Episcopalians years before when he had studied medicine in Edinburgh.

Seabury stayed over a year in England but without result, for there was no way that a bishop could be consecrated for a country not under British rule. Before any consecration the government issued "Letters Patent" which gave a specific area of jurisdiction, besides which the bishop-elect had to take the oath of obedience to the Crown. Obviously the British Government could not give anyone jurisdiction in the United States after the Revolution, and Seabury could not take an oath of obedience to the British Crown. Since the entire journey was undertaken at his own expense, Seabury felt unable to stay longer in England, and accordingly went north to Scotland.

The Episcopal Church in Scotland was still living under a ban, and no public services could be held because their bishops would take no oath of allegiance to any other sovereign than a Stuart. However, the Scottish bishops were quite willing to consecrate Seabury for Connecticut and the service was held at Aberdeen on November 14, 1784, "in the presence of a considerable number of respectable clergymen and a great number of laity." The consecrators were Kilgour, the Primus, Petrie and Skinner. The latter took occasion to say that the Episcopal Church of Scotland had ventured for a long time to show more regard for the Acts of the Apostles than to the Acts of the British Parliament!

Seabury agreed to urge the American Church to use the Scottish liturgy and especially the Prayer of Consecration in the service of Holy Communion. He set forth on the return journey in due course and landed at Newport, Rhode Island, on June 20, 1785. He preached there at Trinity Church the following Sunday and then proceeded to New London, Connecticut, where he became rector of St. James Church. By August he had ordained four men to the diaconate, the first ordinations to be held by an Anglican bishop in North America.

While Seabury was in England in 1784, William White, rector of Christ Church, Philadelphia, called together an informal conference of Churchmen. These delegates who came from seven states decided that a General Convention should be called for September, 1785. White was chosen president of this primary convention, for it speedily became evident that here was a man of great vision and wise statesmanship. He had been ordained in England, had become assistant and then rector of Christ Church, Philadelphia, and was chaplain of the Continental Congress, except for one year, from 1777 to 1800.

Since there were no delegates from Connecticut or Massachusetts, it remained for the delegates from the Middle and Southern States to draft a Constitution, revise the Prayer Book, and plan for an eventual House of Bishops. Connecticut had proceeded on the theory that it was necessary first to obtain the episcopate, while the Convention of 1785 felt the primary need was for a constitution which among other things would define the functions of a bishop in a nonestablished Church.

The federal idea which was adopted for the Constitution was largely the work of White and William Smith. The Church was to be a national organization, of which the dioceses, coterminous with the States, were the component parts. The Convention was to consist of two orders, the clergy and the laity; a triennial General Convention (to which bishops would be admitted!) would have power to legislate for the general welfare of the Church; and the English Book of Common Prayer with certain alterations would be the worship book of the Church.

Unfortunately, the Convention attempted to revise the Prayer Book after only three days of consideration by a committee, followed by four days of debate by the Convention. The results of such hasty action left much to be desired, and the English Archbishops and Bishops to whom the Proposed Book was submitted raised grave objections, especially to the omission of the Nicene Creed. As a result the Nicene Creed was restored, and it was agreed that the English Prayer Book of 1662 should be the standard until a competent committee of General Convention could revise it.

These lengthy negotiations caused the second General Convention of June, 1786, to be adjourned until October of that year. This was the Convention that signed testimonials for Doctors Provoost, White, and Griffiths who had been elected bishops for New York, Pennsylvania, and Virginia respectively. Griffiths was too poor to take the journey to England but Provoost and White went and were duly consecrated at Lambeth Palace Chapel on February 4, 1787, by the Archbishops of Canterbury and York, the Bishop of London and three other bishops. The legal ground had been cleared for this service, for in the previous year Parliament had passed an act authorizing the Archbishops of England "to consecrate persons being subjects or citizens of countries out of His Majesty's dominions." The Church in America now had three bishops and three years later it had four with the consecration in England of James Madison for Virginia. In 1792 all four American bishops, Seabury, Provoost, White, and Madison united in the consecration of Thomas Claggett for Maryland.

The adjourned second General Convention had finished its work on the Constitution and the revision of the Prayer Book by October, 1786, so that the Church was properly equipped to function on its own as an independent branch of the Anglican Communion; and this within only a few years after the end of the Revolution. It was William White's sagacious statesmanship that was largely responsible for this rapid progress, and it is good to record that he lived for nearly fifty years after these events and took part in the consecrations of twenty-seven American bishops, the last being that of Jackson Kemper in 1835.

Unfortunately, while the Church was setting her own house in order on the eastern seaboard, she could give scant attention to the frontier and its missionary possibilities. Four hundred thousand people crossed the Appalachians from 1775 to 1800; they poured through the Hudson-Mohawk depression, they traveled the Susquehanna route, the Forbes road and the Cumberland Gap in the march to Michigan, Wisconsin, Ohio, Indiana, and Illinois. The Church had no settled missionary policy until 1835, and although it tripled its communicant strength in the first thirty-five years of the nineteenth century, the gain was largely along the Atlantic seaboard. Since an official return in 1761 to the Bishop of London had set the Anglican membership in the Colonies as 250,000, it will readily be seen that the war dealt a sad blow to the Church since there were but 30,000 communicants by 1830.[11]

However, new life came with new leadership when John Henry Hobart became coadjutor of New York in 1811 and its diocesan in 1816. Also, in 1811 Philander Chase, returning from his church in New Orleans, settled in the East for a few years before going to Ohio in 1815. He became first Bishop of Ohio in 1819 and performed prodigies of travel and of church upbuilding. He also built a theological seminary, Bexley Hall, and Kenyon College, which he named after their English donors. Chase resigned from Ohio, but after three years of retirement he became first Bishop of Illinois in 1835, and in the next dozen years this indefatigable man had ordained ten deacons and eight priests, consecrated nine churches, baptized two hundred twenty-two, and confirmed four hundred ninety-five persons.

Another outstanding figure was Alexander Viets Griswold who was consecrated with Hobart in 1811 for the Eastern Diocese which included all of New England except Connecticut. He gave wise and steady leadership in an area where the Church was often hated, and the Church grew during his term of office. Likewise, there was new life in Virginia, the Carolinas, Kentucky, and Tennessee.

As it happened, the Church, which was on the threshold of a great continental missionary awakening, conducted its first notable missionary adventure in Europe. On January 1, 1829, the Reverend John Jacob Robertson set sail from New York for Greece. He went under the auspices of a missionary society organized under the presidency of Bishop William White, and for some years gave aid to the Greek Church, which had recently freed itself from Turkish rule. Dr. Robertson was transferred to Constantinople in 1839, and he there established the "Oriental Mission." The following year Robertson was joined by the Reverend Horatio Southgate, who subsequently was consecrated bishop for this Oriental Mission in 1844.

It was the General Convention of 1835 which made the great missionary decision to send bishops to the West without waiting to be asked, and Jackson Kemper became the first such missionary sent to represent the whole Church. He had been West to Pittsburgh and Wisconsin in previous years, so he knew something of the problems that would face him as Bishop of Indiana and Missouri, with additional pioneer work in Iowa, Minnesota and Wisconsin, Kansas and Nebraska. The first railroad in the East was then but six years old, and while one could go from the western end of

Lake Erie to Chicago or Cincinnati by rail, the steamboat and horses were Kemper's main means of transportation.

The election of bishops for Missouri, Indiana, Iowa, Minnesota, and Kansas between 1849 and 1864 left Kemper free to concentrate on Wisconsin, and he became the bishop of that state from 1854 until his death sixteen years later. By this time Kemper had traveled over three hundred thousand miles, and the seventy clergy and more than ten thousand other persons who attended his funeral bore witness to his outstanding influence. The Church could produce great missionaries, but never enough of them soon enough to be strongly entrenched in the middle and far West. Bishop William I. Kip had gone to Califorina in 1853, and Bishop Thomas Scott went to the Oregon Territory the next year.

The horror of the Civil War caused a temporary split in the Episcopal Church, but only for the duration of the struggle. At the Convention of 1865 representatives from the border states, and Texas and North Carolina answered the roll call and the brief schism was over. The Church continued to grow so that by the end of the century it numbered some 750,000 communicants.

At least three notable bishops belong to this era. Henry Benjamin Whipple, elected to Minnesota in 1859, became the great friend of the Indians and was put on the Board of Indian Commissioners in 1869 by President Grant. At the time of his death in 1901, he was perhaps the most widely known ecclesiastic in the American Church. Queen Victoria thought so much of him that he was offered the bishopric of the Sandwich Islands (Hawaii) in 1871. Another outstanding man was William Hobart Hare, who began a remarkable missionary episcopate in the Dakota Territory in 1873. The large numbers of Sioux who are Episcopalians today is due to the firm foundation laid by the frail and cultured man from the East who did such a magnificent work in the West.

Daniel Sylvester Tuttle belongs also to this saga of western expansion. He became Bishop of Montana with jurisdiction of Idaho and Utah in 1867, a time when it took twenty-five days to go by passenger coach from St. Joseph, Missouri, to the Pacific Coast. The Homestead Act of 1862 had increased migrations west of the Mississippi, while the completion of the transcontinental railroad seven years later made the westward shift of population much easier and more rapid. Tuttle surveyed his vast jurisdiction going by way of Salt Lake City to Virginia City and Helena, Montana. In those days travel was both dangerous and expensive. Tuttle often slept with a gun under his pillow, and he paid a fare of one hundred twenty dollars for the four hundred mile journey from Salt Lake to Boise! New missionary districts were taken from Tuttle's jurisdiction from time to time so that by 1890, when the Diocese of West Missouri was formed from Missouri, his administrative area was reduced from an original 340,000 to 32,000 square miles. Tuttle was Presiding Bishop from 1903 until his death twenty years later.

A significant overhauling of the Church's organization began in 1919 when General Convention provided for the election of the Presiding Bishop, who until then had been the senior and often the most feeble member of the House of Bishops. By another quarter century the Church would release its Presiding Bishop from his diocese and make him as much of an archbishop and metropolitan as possible, given the inherited prejudices of American churchmen. Also, in 1919, the National Council was organized to carry on the Church's work between General Conventions. Besides its president who is the Presiding Bishop, and other officers, the

58

Council consists of twenty-eight bishops, priests, and laity, elected by General Convention and by the Provinces. It is not precisely the executive committee of General Convention, but increasingly it is the interim directing body of the Church's total program. Joint Commissions of General Convention also carry on major interests between Conventions.

The Church has made notable contributions to the cause of Christian reunion, by enunciating the famous Chicago Quadrilateral of 1886 and by contributing notable leaders such as Bishop Charles Henry Brent, who was president of the first World Conference on Faith and Order in Lausanne in 1927. It has also contributed two presidents to the Federal Council of Churches, and one president to the National Council of Churches of Christ in the United States of America, and one president of the World Council of Churches.

The Episcopal Church gained a million members from 1938 to 1956, and though it continues to exert an influence out of proportion to its total membership, it is still very much a minority church. Compared with other Anglican Churches, it has certainly manifested notable ability in its organization and overall administrative effectiveness. On the other hand its total overseas missionary program is quite small compared with the potential of the home base, and many of its members do not realize that they belong to the Anglican Communion.

THE MISSIONARY DISTRICT
OF ALASKA

Alaska owes its discovery to the Danish navigator Vitus Bering, who sailed from Kamchatka to Alaska in 1741 while he was in the employ of the Russian government. Later in the century (1794) Russian missionaries visited the Kodiak

Islands and baptized several thousands there, and in 1824 the remarkable Russian Orthodox priest, John Veniaminoff, went to Unalaska, one of the Aleutians. He later became bishop of the Orthodox diocese of Okhotsk and Kamchatka when it was organized in 1840. Official government support of the Church was withdrawn after 1867, but three years later a diocese of Alaska and the Aleutians was organized and a bishop appointed.[12]

The appointment of a Russian governor for Alaska in 1861 made the United States government realize the importance of acquiring this territory, which Seward finally purchased in 1867 for a little more than seven million dollars. As a consequence, the last non-British European power left North America. The population of the country in those days was less then thirty thousand, of whom two-thirds were Eskimo. Archdeacon MacDonald of the Canadian Church began a mission at Fort Yukon in 1862, five years before the purchase; it was not until much later, in 1889, that an American priest, the Reverend John W. Chapman, arrived at Anvik on the Yukon where he labored faithfully for many years. The General Convention of the Episcopal Church, meeting in Minneapolis in 1895, elected the Reverend Peter Trimble Rowe, rector of Sault Sainte Marie, as first Missionary Bishop of Alaska which had been made a Missionary District three years before. When Rowe arrived in his jurisdiction he found work going on at three points, Anvik under Chapman, Point Hope under Dr. Driggs, and Tanana under the Reverend J. L. Prevost. Rowe served for forty-seven years, during which time he built thirty-seven churches and seven hospitals. He travelled his vast territory by snowshoe, dog team, boat, and, in his later years, by airplane. At the time of his death in 1942 Rowe was one of the most famous missionaries of the Anglican Church.

Another well known missionary was the Venerable Hudson Stuck, who gave up the deanship of the Cathedral at Dallas to go to Alaska to help Bishop Rowe. Stuck became Archdeacon of the Yukon and, like his chief, he spent many years in arduous travel. Perhaps his most spectacular accomplishment was the scaling of the hitherto unscaled Mount McKinley with three companions in 1913. A church hospital at Fort Yukon, named after Hudson Stuck, served for almost forty years by another devoted medical missionary, Grafton Burke, who saw the town grow from the "worst hellhole in Alaska" to a fine community. The hospital has recently closed because the government has now established hospitals throughout Alaska.

Rowe was succeeded by his suffragan, John B. Bentley, in 1942; the latter resigned six years later to become vice-president of the National Council with charge of all the Church's work overseas. The present bishop, William J. Gordon, has become famous as the bishop who travels by his plane, *The Blue Box,* given him from the United Thank Offering of the Woman's Auxiliary of the Episcopal Church.

THE ANGLICAN CHURCH OF CANADA

Long before Christ lived Greek philosophers surmised that water surrounded the world. But the honor of discovering that there was water for at least three thousand miles west of Europe probably belongs to Leif Ericsson. In all likelihood he landed somewhere on the eastern shore of what is now Canada or the United States about A.D. 1000.

Almost five centuries later, in 1497, the Cabots, representing the parsimonious Henry VII of England, sailed from Bristol with a British crew and landed on the coast of Labrador. They were the first of many pioneers who tried for three and a half centuries to find a northwest passage to the Far East. Martin Frobisher, fired with this objective, crossed the Atlantic to Baffin Land in 1578, and while there his Anglican chaplain celebrated the Holy Communion. Henry Hudson's explorations were likewise undertaken to find the passage but he, too, was unsuccessful and his adventurous life ended on the southeast corner of Hudson's Bay in 1611, where he was cast adrift by his mutinous crew. These early explorations were important both geographically and politically, for not only did the adventurers often claim the newly discovered territory for their financial backers, they also had the incentive of large rewards offered for the discovery of a sea passage to India and China. As late as 1745 the British Parliament offered a reward of twenty thousand pounds for the one who discovered such a northwest passage, but no one succeeded until modern times.

Nova Scotia, called *Acadie* by the French, was ceded to Great Britain by the Treaty of Utrecht in 1713, and at the same time the Hudson's Bay territory was declared to be a British possession. Regular church services had been held at Annapolis Royal in Nova Scotia since 1710, but the first Anglican Church in Canada was not built until 1750 at the newly founded town of Halifax where English, Germans, and Dutch made their home. By 1758 the Crown had established the Church in Nova Scotia, which meant that in each township four hundred acres of land were set apart for the clergyman's glebe, as well as two hundred acres for the schoolmaster. Actually, from 1763, the British Government intended to establish by law the Church of England in Lower Canada (Quebec) and Upper Canada (Ontario).

The Treaty of Paris, in 1763, secured all of Canada and the rest of the Maritime Provinces for Great Britain although the population at the time was still largely French and would probably have remained so except for the American Revolution. This latter event caused tens of thousands of United Empire Loyalists, as they were called, to migrate to New Brunswick and Upper Canada (Ontario), where they founded Kingston and other towns. The British Government assisted them generously with land, food, and clothing, and after the British defeat at Saratoga many more thousands of Loyalists crossed the border. S.P.G. sent a missionary to St. John's, New Brunswick, in 1785 and the new Anglican colony flourished there.

The need for a bishop for Canada was becoming more and more apparent, and in March, 1783, Samuel Seabury and Charles Inglis met in New York to plan for a bishop for Nova Scotia. Some three years later Inglis was chosen bishop, and he was consecrated in England as Bishop of Nova Scotia and the Dependencies on August 12, 1787. His diocese, which consisted of Nova Scotia, New Brunswick, Prince Edward Island, Lower Canada (Quebec), Upper Canada (Ontario) and Newfoundland, was subject to the Archbishop of Canterbury. Thus two priceless benefits came to the Anglican Church in Canada as a result of the Revolutionary War: tens of thousands of Anglicans and a bishop.

Inglis, an Irishman, had worked in the American colonies as rector of Trinity Church in New York during the War of Independence. On one occasion during the struggle, a hundred armed rebels entered his church during divine service with drums beating and fifes playing, and sought to dissuade

63

Inglis from reading the prayer for the King. In spite of this Inglis carried on with the service with an even voice and undisturbed mien. His episcopate was a notable one, for he possessed great vision and had deep insight into human character and the needs of the infant Church in Canada. He founded an academy at Windsor in 1788, and later King's College, which in 1926 was moved to Halifax. It is the oldest chartered university in the overseas British Commonwealth, and it did a great deal to meet the need for clergy and educated laymen throughout the years. During Inglis' first visitation he covered more than seven hundred miles and confirmed more than five hundred persons; he died in 1816 after a very fruitful episcopate of twenty-nine years.

The consecration of Jacob Mountain as first Bishop of Quebec in 1793 began the westward expansion of an organized Church, and in his twenty-two years of leadership, his clergy grew from nine to seventy-three, and the number of church buildings rose from six to sixty. This latter included the first Cathedral to be erected outside the British Isles, Holy Trinity, Quebec. It was built by the Royal Engineers, having been ordered by George III in 1800 at the expense of the Crown. It was consecrated four years later.

Bishop Jacob Mountain's successor to the See of Quebec was Bishop Charles James Stewart, a son of the Earl of Galloway, who had come out to Canada as a missionary in 1807 and took over the difficult task of founding a mission at St. Armand. He arrived in town on a Saturday night and was immediately warned by the landlord of the local inn that there would be a riot if he tried to hold services on the morrow. Not to be intimidated, Stewart replied, "Then here is the place for me." So the services were held, and in ten years he had a flourishing Church. Stewart was consecrated in

64

1826 for Quebec with oversight of Upper Canada (Ontario) as well. He continued to administer this vast area until the year of his death, when a son of the former bishop was made coadjutor for Montreal.

The population of Ontario farther west was increasing by leaps and bounds, and had doubled in the decade 1826 to 1835. When John Strachan became the first Bishop of Toronto in 1839, the organized Church was moved several hundred miles farther west. This was considerable progress since Inglis' consecration a little over fifty years before. Nor was the East forgotten, because John Medley became the first Bishop of Fredericton, New Brunswick, in 1845, his support coming largely from the newly-established Colonial Bishoprics Fund in England.

Bishop Strachan is the key figure of this era, for he was not only a man of marked ability but had an episcopate of forty years. He had been in Canada since 1799, he knew well the Church's need for clergy, for Christian education, and for self-government, and he did much for all three needs. It was largely due to his efforts that King's College, Toronto, was founded with a royal charter that gave the Church control, but this control was lost in 1848 by an act of the Legislature, and the institution became the secular University of Toronto. Not to be daunted by this grave loss, the Bishop immediately set about to obtain a new charter and money for building Trinity College in 1851.

It was in this same year that Bishop Strachan held a significant meeting of clergy and laymen at Holy Trinity Church, Toronto. This was the first meeting of a synod type to be held within the Empire and it marked a notable step towards self-government in the Church. It should be remembered that until 1832 the Church was a State Church,

65

its bishops were creatures of the State, and many clergy were paid by the government. From the latter year onwards gradual disestablishment took place; and by 1852 all State support was discontinued by legislative act. This meant self-support for the Church, but it meant also that the Church had the right to govern its own affairs. Accordingly, in 1852 the diocese of Toronto organized as a Synod, and in 1854 Bishop Mountain founded the Synod of Quebec. In 1857 the Canadian Legislature made diocesan and provincial synods legal, and in the same year a conference of the bishops of North America was called at Quebec for the purpose of establishing these organs of autonomy. The transition from a State church to a self-governing one may be illustrated by the way three contemporary bishops were consecrated: Benjamin Cronyn, chosen for Huron in 1857, was elected in Canada and consecrated in England; Dr. J. T. Lewis was elected in Canada in 1862, and was consecrated at Kingston, Ontario, although the Queen issued Letters Patent; Dr. A. N. Bethune was elected in Toronto in 1867, and consecrated in Canada without the royal license. These mark important steps in the contraction of the power of the Crown and the growing independence of the Canadian Church. Nor was the provincial organization neglected, for the five dioceses of Nova Scotia, Quebec, Fredericton, Montreal, and Rupert's Land united to form a Province in 1860, seven years before the British North-American Act when the secular provinces entered a Confederation and established a Dominion Government at Ottawa.

During these years of consolidation and movement towards autonomy, the Church was moving farther west and north. One main route to the Northwest was by way of Hudson's Bay. The Company of that name had been engaged in the

66

fur trade since the end of the seventeenth century, and the terms of its 1670 charter gave it almost complete control over an area as large as the Roman Empire; its influence stretched from Ontario to the Pacific and from the border of the United States to the Arctic Circle. It is good to record that the Company pursued an enlightened policy towards missionary work for its own men, for the Indians, and for the Eskimos farther north. A really notable saga of Christian missions in Canada began when the Reverend John West went to Rupert's Land in 1820 preaching and teaching the Christian faith to all who would listen. Much of the traveling over his vast parish had to be done on foot, and on one occasion he walked one hundred and eighty miles to visit an Eskimo village. So great was his success that it may be said truthfully that he laid permanent foundations for the Church's later success with the Eskimo. Another tireless traveler of this era was Bishop George Mountain who sat in an open canoe during a thirty-two day voyage in 1844 when he visited the western portion of his diocese. It can be readily understood why Mountain, when he returned, recommended that another bishop be appointed to care for the distant and growing western area. Accordingly, David Anderson became first Bishop of Rupert's Land in 1849, and some idea of its vastness may be gathered from the fact that two of his clergy could not get to a meeting he called in 1860, because one was 2500 miles to the northwest at Fort Simpson and another was 1250 miles to the east at Moose! In time this diocese became the mother of ten other dioceses in the West.

However, "the power of a man and the power of a moment" in history came together in the episcopate of Robert Machray from 1865 to 1904. This was the time of a great westward expansion and the period when the Canadian Pacific Railway was abuilding. The full-bearded Scot who took charge of Rupert's Land at this period remains not only one of the great missionary leaders of the Canadian Church, but one of the most notable in the Anglican Communion. He threw himself into the problems of self-support, he revived St. John's College for training men for the ministry, he did much for primary education, and he held a synod of his clergy and laity in 1869. Very appropriately he came to know two notable American missionary bishops, who were his neighbors to the South, Whipple of Minnesota, and Kemper of Wisconsin. These he met first when on his way to the General Convention of the American Church in New York in 1868, where he had been invited to celebrate the Holy Communion at the opening service.

Machray secured the interest of the Archbishop of Canterbury in the erection of three new dioceses for the prairie provinces and in the appointment of bishops for them. John Horden was consecrated for Moosonee in 1872, and John McLean for Saskatchewan and William Carpenter Bompas for Athabasca in 1874. Horden had come to Moose Fort in 1851 when the entire Indian population was pagan, and when both witchcraft and cannibalism were practiced. He learned the Cree language as well as many others, and translated the Bible and Prayer Book into Cree. McLean's diocese embraced the fast growing wheat areas of plainland up to the Rocky Mountains, while Bompas' huge diocese of more than 600,000 square miles was later subdivided twice, with Bompas each time taking the more remote area. He died, suddenly and quietly, while writing a sermon in 1904, after a singularly fruitful life and work. He has rightfully been called "The Apostle of the North." With all these developments, Machray retained the See of Rupert's Land, now considerably diminished in size, and became its first Metropolitan, and in 1893 Primate of All Canada.

The Church did not reach the Pacific Coast until the middle nineteenth century, and only after that section of the country had gone through a varied history. Vancouver Island was leased to the Hudson's Bay Company in 1843, attached as a Crown Colony in 1849, united with British Columbia in 1866, and incorporated with the Dominion of Canada five years later. The first Anglican clergyman in those parts was one R. G. Staines, a Hudson's Bay chaplain, who went there in 1849. Fortunately, due to a generous private endowment of the Baroness Burdett-Coutts, the territory obtained a bishop in 1859, and after another decade two other bishops were consecrated for New Westminster and Caledonia. To-day Anglicans number one-third of the population of the Province.

The First General Synod of the Church was not held until 1893 in Toronto, but the birth of the Dominion in 1867 and the completion of the Canadian Pacific Railroad in 1885 did much to point to the need for closer relationships between the dioceses and provinces. When Machray was elected Primate and Metropolitan and when J. T. Lewis of Ontario became Archbishop of Canada, these two, together with Nuttall of Jamaica, were the first archbishops of the Anglican Church outside the British Isles. It was becoming evident that, as the Church achieved self-government, it also needed the cohesiveness of the provincial system.

There are four provinces in the Canadian Church: Canada, Ontario, Rupert's Land, and British Columbia. The Province of Canada has five dioceses, including Newfoundland. Quebec, which is in this province, contains 85% Roman Catholics. Ontario, where the people are largely Anglo-Saxon and where the Anglican Church is strongest, has eight dioceses. Rupert's Land has ten dioceses, and is still largely a prairie and missionary country. British Columbia has six dioceses, and here the population is 25% Anglican. Each province has an Archbishop who is elected by the province, while the Primate and Metropolitan is elected from among the bishops and archbishops.

Taking its inspiration from the American Church, the Woman's Auxiliary was begun in 1885, and it has given great impetus to the entire missionary program of the Church. Another significant moment came in 1902 when the Missionary Society of the Church in Canada was born at the General Synod; for the first time it was stated officially that all baptized members of the Church belonged to the Missionary Society.

The Church in Canada has the distinction of having the largest diocese in the whole of the Anglican Church, for the Diocese of the Arctic covers two and a quarter million square miles, or one and a quarter million square miles excluding the water (or ice) areas. This tremendous jurisdiction was created in 1933 for the purpose of bringing all the Eskimo work under one bishop. Eighty-two per cent of the total Arctic population of 8,500 are Anglican and many of them are trained as catechists and lay readers. Thievery, lying, and infanticide were once quite accepted customs amongst the Eskimos; but the Church, which has been working in the Arctic since the eighteen-twenties, has lifted them to a new level. Many of them are very faithful to their Church, and it is not uncommon even today to hear that Eskimos have traveled two hundred miles to an Easter service.

Newfoundland is the latest diocese to be added to the Anglican Church in Canada. It was originally under the jurisdiction of Inglis as we have seen, but it was made a separate diocese in 1839. Bishop Feild is the great name associated with this diocese from 1844 to 1875. Not only did he travel extensively around the coast and to Labrador in his fifty-ton schooner, *Hawk;* he also began a cathedral and a seminary, and raised a diocesan endowment. In 1949 Newfoundland became a part of the Anglican Church of Canada, and was attached to the Province of Canada.

The Church has eleven theological schools, somewhat more perhaps than the size of the present Church warrants. Since some of these are relatively small and poor, much might be gained by consolidation.

With regard to the question of reunion, the General Synod issued invitations to other Christian bodies in 1943 to discuss the possibilities of reunion. This invitation led to a series of discussions with the United Church of Canada which continue in spite of grave problems, particularly concerning the nature of the ministry.

The Canadian Church used the Church of England 1662 Prayer Book until it undertook a mild revision of the latter in 1918. A new committee began work in 1943, and a Draft Prayer Book was presented at General Synod in 1950, which comes back for final approval in 1958. The new proposed Kalendar includes names of notable Christians, as being worthy of remembrance without claiming sainthood for them. Laud, Latimer, Ridley, More, King Charles I, Ken, Hooker, Simeon, and Keble are there, as are also the martyr bishops, Hannington and Patteson, and Canadian pioneer bishops, Inglis and Horden, and a priest, John West.

At the General Synod of 1955, the Church happily changed its name from the Church of England in Canada to the Angli can Church of Canada. It would be a great deal less confusing

71

if all the Anglican Churches made a similar change in their official names. More important than the name is the fact that the Anglican Church of Canada has been notable for its vigorous missionary work, for its sound, conservative worship, and for its growing reputation for scholarship. In recent years it has largely outgrown an earlier undue reliance on the Mother Church for supplying its top leadership.

THE CHURCH OF THE PROVINCE
OF THE WEST INDIES

The Church of the Province of the West Indies comprises eight dioceses, six of which are islands or groups of islands in the Caribbean Sea, while one is in Central America, and one on the north coast of South America. These Caribbean islands and colonies came under British rule over a period of some three hundred years. Their effective government posed difficult problems due to the generally unhealthy climate and the large slave populations. However, the West Indies assumed added importance to England after the loss of the American Colonies, and, indeed, without them England's long struggle with Napoleon could never have succeeded.

There were no dioceses and the Church was very weak here during the slavery period, for there were only about fifty clergy on the Islands in those days. These men were in no sense a group under authority but rather a number of individuals partly under the authority of the local governor and partly under the tenuous control of the Bishop of London. The fact that there were no bishops meant that there was no effective ecclesiastical authority, and there was little if any desire on the part of the clergy to teach the slaves anything about the Christian faith. The British slave trade with the

West Indies had begun towards the end of the sixteenth century, and it has been estimated that between 1680 and 1786 some two million slaves were brought over from West Africa. This slave population of the Islands became increasingly difficult for the whites to deal with, and there were many bloody rebellions over the years. The sad fact is that these slaves in British possessions lived in "unrelieved heathenism" until shortly before the Emancipation, and the Church in the West Indies had to wait until 1824 before bishops were consecrated for Barbados and Jamaica. This was in unhappy contrast to Nova Scotia which had received its first bishop thirty-seven years before. As it happened the first two bishops in the West Indies had but ten years in which to prepare their large dioceses for the impact of Emancipation in 1834.

In this year the Emancipation Act gave freedom to all slaves within the Empire, and their owners were paid twenty million pounds indemnity. It was provided in the Act that all slaves then under six years old and all born subsequent to the Act were free; all others were to become free four years hence. So, on August 1, 1838, eight hundred thousand West Indians obtained their freedom; or as Bishop Lipscombe said at the time, "Eight hundred thousand human beings lay down at night as slaves and rose in the morning as free as ourselves."

Fortunately, ten years before this, the Church had erected the Dioceses of Barbados and Jamaica to obtain episcopal supervision for the West Indies; in the course of time six other dioceses grew from the original two, between 1842 and 1883. In the order of their foundation they are: Barbados and Jamaica, 1824; Guiana and Antigua, 1842; Nassau, 1862; Trinidad, 1872; Windward Islands, 1878; and British Honduras, 1883.

Barbados, founded in 1824, had as its first diocesan the notable William Hart Coleridge, scion of a distinguished family in England. The island of Barbados had become a British colony in 1605, and twenty-two years later Lord Carlisle was granted a patent wherein his lordship was instructed to use the grant "for propagating the Christian faith" as well as for "enlarging His Majesty's dominions." Although the Bishop of London had jurisdiction in those days, in point of fact the civil governors actually exercised both political and ecclesiastical authority, for they even appointed clergy to vacant parishes until well into the nineteenth century.

Long before it had become a diocese the Church in Barbados was greatly blessed through the will of General Christopher Codrington, a former Governor of the Leeward Islands, who retired to Barbados and finally died there on Good Friday in 1710. Codrington left all his estates in Barbados and a sizable fortune, to S.P.G. for the purpose of founding a college in Barbados to train men for the ministry. In his bequest the good general directed that the future students were not only to take vows of poverty, chastity, and obedience, but they were also to learn the practice of medicine so they might heal men's bodies as well as their souls. Legal battles over the will ensued but S.P.G. finally came into possession of the estate. A school for boys was begun first, and by 1831 it was possible to admit theological students. Since that time Codrington Missionary Training College has had a distinguished history, not only in providing native clergy for the West Indies but also in helping the "Pongas Mission" in West Africa, a project begun by Principal Richard Rawle in 1851. Rawle, who directed Codrington from 1847 to 1864, was a most distinguished missionary and teacher and at one time it was contemplated seriously that he should succeed Selwyn

74

in New Zealand. Codrington has continued its valuable work to the present day and is currently directed by the Community of the Resurrection.

When William Hart Coleridge was consecrated the first bishop for Barbados with jurisdiction in the Leeward Islands, Trinidad, and Guiana, he discovered that the Barbadians had remained in large measure loyal to the Anglican Church in spite of their never having had episcopal supervision. Both Coleridge and Lipscombe (who was consecrated at the same time for Jamaica) had to address themselves to two great problems, the supervision of the clergy and the instruction of the slave population in preparation for the latter's eventual freedom. When Emancipation came in 1834, the four years of transition to 1838 proved to be much too short a time for educating the former slaves to freedom, but S.P.G. poured in both men and money to help the bishops in this anxious time, and the Society spent not less than one hundred seventy-two thousand pounds on this project alone.

The Church was established in Barbados in 1824, but when disestablishment came in 1870 to it and to other dioceses, the Barbadians promptly set up an established Church of their own. So it remains to this day, the only established Church in the Anglican Communion outside the Church of England. A synod was formed in 1911, but the Legislature has the final authority over it, and the bishop and clergy are paid from public funds.

Jamaica. Oliver Cromwell's arms, somewhat modified, are still the arms of Jamaica, because the Island was captured by Admiral Penn and General Venables in Cromwell's time (1655). Jamaica has been the scene of more than one stirring incident and the famous Admiral Benbow, who died of wounds at Port Royal in 1702, lies buried in Kingston parish churchyard.

During the Spanish rule from 1509 to the middle of the seventeenth century the native population became almost extinct, and the demand for labor on the plantations was such that Jamaica soon became the biggest slave market in the world. Moreover, the Island was not far from Haiti and the slave insurrections there caused repercussions in Jamaica. In 1824 when Bishop Lipscombe arrived in his diocese, which also included the Bahamas and Honduras, he had to face a potential political revolution. The Assembly was so incensed at the prospects of emancipation that they considered seriously whether to declare their independence from Great Britain, or ask the United States to annex them. In addition to this problem the Bishop had also to deal with recalcitrant clergy who were not accustomed to episcopal oversight; he likewise had to deal with the Governor, who insisted on continuing his custom of naming clergy to vacant parishes. In spite of these difficulties the Bishop managed to build thirteen new churches and increase his clergy list from thirty to forty-five. Christian instruction was also commenced for the slaves on two hundred and eighty plantations.

A big population shift occurred towards the end of the nineteenth century, when many thousands of Anglican Jamaicans left for work on the banana plantations in Central America. These were followed by thousands more who were needed for work on the Panama Canal. By 1909 there were more than 30,000 of them in this latter area. The West Indies has always suffered from cyclones, and some islands have had earthquakes; a particularly vicious cyclone hit Jamaica in 1903, which caused great havoc and destroyed most of the churches. It was followed four years later by an earthquake

76

which reduced Kingston to rubble; but again the churches were rebuilt, due in large measure to a gift from the Pan Anglican Congress Thank Offering and to generous private donations from English Churchmen.

In contrast to Barbados, Jamaica has retained only faint vestiges of the former State control in that the final court of appeal for the Church is to an English Committee of Reference; also the Church's constitution, drawn up in 1870, was authorized by the Jamaican Legislature.

Guiana. Guiana, taken from Barbados, became a diocese in 1842, and today the jurisdiction comprises Venezuela together with Dutch and British Guiana. The Dutch had made the first European settlements here in 1613, while the British did not make good their claim to this part of the South American coast until 1815. As a result the British shared the original establishment of the Church in Guiana with the Presbyterian and the Dutch Reformed Churches. The British divided their areas of work into three sections, Essequibo, Demarara, and Berbice; the S.P.G. sponsored a successful mission to the Arawak Indians. The great hero of the period was William Henry Brett, who worked faithfully for forty years and reduced four of the local dialects to writing.

The population is very mixed and consists of Africans, East Indians, Chinese, Madeira Portuguese, and several tribes of Amerindians together with British and American residents. In British Guiana Hindus and Moslems form some 40% of the population, while only 8% is Christian. Much of the hinterland awaits exploration.

As was the case with the other dioceses, disestablishment came in 1870. A new church constitution was adopted in spite of the vigorous opposition of the clergy who objected to the

inclusion of laity in the new Synod. The Synod has full legislative power, and the State has no authority over the Church.
An interesting feature is that the bishop can veto any synodal
legislation, and he also controls the appointments of all the
clergy.

Antigua, Nassau, and Trinidad. Antigua became a diocese in
1842 on its separation from Barbados. When Bishop D. G.
Davies arrived for his enthronement, he found that an earthquake had destroyed the church that was to be his cathedral.
Nassau was taken from Jamaica in 1862 and within its territory is San Salvador where Columbus landed. Trinidad
diocese was erected in 1872. It had been acquired by treaty
in 1797, but the predominant population was French at the
time. Some 18,000 French immigrants arrived here between
1783 and 1797, and the British Government granted them
complete religious freedom. Today the population is largely
Negro and Hindu. Antigua, Nassau and the Bahamas, and
Trinidad all have their own synodal government.

Windward Islands and British Honduras. The last two dioceses to be formed were the Windward Islands in 1878 and
British Honduras in 1883. Honduras at first took the Bishop
of Jamaica for its diocesan, but in 1880 Archbishop of Canterbury Tait asked Bishop Nuttall to organize a separate diocese.
By 1894 the jurisdiction extended from British Guiana to
Costa Rica, but in 1906 the American Church took over the
latter area. Since then the new American diocese of Central
America has caused a major re-arrangement of jurisdictions.

As the years went on, it became obvious that this whole
area would benefit greatly by becoming a Province. Archbishop Tait advised the Bishops of the West Indies to discuss

78

this very matter, and in 1873 they and certain representatives met at Georgetown, British Guiana, to plan for provincial status. This became an accomplished fact by 1880, and shortly thereafter Bishop Austin of British Guiana was elected the first Primate. In 1897 it was decided that the Primate would be given the title of Archbishop and Metropolitan. Any bishop of the Province is eligible for election as Archbishop.

The great distances to be covered have hindered the development of the Province until recently; now the airplane has solved the question of distances—but not of finances. Provincial Synod is still restricted to the bishops for financial reasons, and until recently their Lordships found it easier and cheaper to meet either in London or New York than anywhere in the West Indies. In 1947 there was held a significant meeting of the Bishops of the Church of the Province of the West Indies together with Missionary Bishops from Cuba, Haiti, Canal Zone, and Mexico. A pre-Lambeth meeting, it issued a notable encyclical "Letter to the Faithful." [13] The whole Caribbean area might well be made into one Province combining the American work with the present Province of the West Indies.

The Church in the West Indies runs a rather large number of elementary schools, although the tremendous burden of supporting them makes for a tendency to turn them over to the government. The Church also has taken a leading part in secondary education, and of these schools Kingston College, Jamaica, founded in 1925, is an excellent example. Codrington College has been already mentioned, but there is another institution, St. Peter's Theological College, Jamaica, which has graduated a large number of teachers and clergy. It was built by Bishop Nuttall. Over the years both S.P.G. and S.P.C.K. have given generously to all of these educational ventures. Two communities of religious are at work in the West Indies, the Sisters of St. Peter, who are in Nassau, and the Community of the Companions of Jesus the Good Shepherd, whose work lies in Barbados, Antigua, Guiana, and Honduras.

Overpopulation, with its accompanying poverty, is the most pressing problem in the West Indies. Two illustrations will suffice: Jamaica's population of more than 1,300,000 attempts to subsist on 4,000 square miles of limestone rock and eroded hillsides; and even so the population continues to grow at the rate of 29,000 a year! In the Leeward Islands, there were 200 people to the square mile eighty-five years ago; now there are 422 to the square mile!

The Church has no Prayer Book of its own, although work is currently proceeding on a West Indian Liturgy. Until this is accomplished, any diocesan may use the Book of 1549, the Book of 1662, or an Interim Rite drawn up and approved by the Synod of the Province.

THE MISSIONARY DIOCESE OF BERMUDA

The Bermudas, sometimes called the Somers Islands, were named after Sir George Somers, who was wrecked on a Bermudian reef while on his way to the Colonies in 1609. The Islands had been discovered by Spaniards a hundred years before, but no colonization had taken place. Two trading companies used Bermuda, and in 1620 a representative government was set up; it functioned until 1684 when the Islands became a Crown Colony, the second oldest such colony in the Commonwealth.

Bermuda was the place selected by Dean, afterwards Bishop, George Berkeley for his projected missionary college that was to serve the American colonies with a steady supply of clergy. The failure of his plan, due to Walpole's double dealing, had profound effects in the American Church in the colonies, for Berkeley returned home in 1731, abandoned his plan, and became Bishop of Cloyne shortly thereafter.

S.P.G. began work in Bermuda in 1822, and three years afterwards it became an archdeaconry of Nova Scotia, whose Bishop Spencer visited the Islands in the following year. As a result of this visit, the colonial legislature formed eight parishes on the inhabited islands and provided four clergy livings. Bishop Spencer confirmed twelve hundred persons on his initial visitation.

The ten mission schools which were shortly established were invaluable from 1838 onwards when all the slaves were freed and so much needed to be done to help them use their freedom properly. The following year, 1839, when the Diocese of Newfoundland was created, Bermuda was attached to it, and this relationship continued until 1917 when a separate diocese was established. Bermuda has had its own bishop since 1925.

THE MISSIONARY DISTRICTS IN THE CARIBBEAN

Cuba. Cuba, Santo Domingo, and Puerto Rico were all discovered by Columbus and became part of the Spanish or French Empires until the decline of those powers at the end of the eighteenth century. Cuba had been used as a base for explorations to Mexico, Yucatan, and Florida in the sixteenth century, and as early as 1523 West African slaves began to supply Cuba and the other chief islands with cheap labor to replace the vanishing natives.

The first Anglican service on the Island appears to have

been held in a Franciscan chapel in 1762, and while there were doubtless many other sporadic services held at various times, a settled priest did not come until 1876, when Bishop Henry Benjamin Whipple of Minnesota sent Edward Kenny to Cuba's foreign colony. The ubiquitous Bishop of Minnesota had visited the Island in 1871 on his way to Haiti. Kenny did notable missionary work for fifteen years, especially during the recurrent yellow fever epidemics. There were doubtless great opportunities awaiting the Church, for when Bishop John F. Young of Florida visited Cuba in 1885, he confirmed 325 persons. Cuba became an independent nation in 1899 and the interest of the American Church in Cuba increased over the next few years; in 1901 the Island was organized as a Missionary District and a bishop, Albion W. Knight, was consecrated for it in 1904.

A number of missions had been started by this time, perhaps the most notable being that at Matanzas under Sr. Pedro Duarte, a former Roman Catholic, who also began a parochial school there. Bishop Knight was able to report that he had a staff of ten clergy and more than four hundred communicants two years after he began his work in 1905. Fifty years later there were almost sixty thousand baptized members.

The fifteen parochial schools over the Island have done much to bring about these results. Also, many Anglicans in Cuba are now second and third generation, which means that they are more stable in the Faith. The great majority of the five million Cubans are Roman Catholic, but the Episcopal Church has grown significantly under the leadership of Bishop Hugo Blankingship since 1939. Holy Trinity Cathedral, Havana, consecrated on St. Andrew's Day, 1947, has attached to it a fine parochial school. There is also a large girls' school, Sarah Ashurst, at Guantanamo.

Haiti and the Dominican Republic. Haiti was the most prosperous of the West Indian islands until the French Revolution, when the French National Assembly decreed equal rights for both Negro and white people in 1791. Toussaint L'Ouverture became master of the island by another decade, and he ruled with wisdom and firmness. And at the same time he resisted boldly Napoleon's attempt to re-introduce slavery. L'Ouverture was finally captured by the French and sent to France, where he died in 1802. Two years after this Haiti proclaimed its independence.

After the Civil War, the American government was looking for places besides Liberia to which former slaves might be sent, and so it happened that more than a hundred migrated to Haiti led by an American Negro, James Theodore Holly, who had recently been ordained. The American Church Missionary Society assisted with this initial Anglican mission in 1861, and five years later the Board of Missions of the Episcopal Church took it over. Holly proved to be so able a leader that he was elected and consecrated Bishop of the "Orthodox Apostolic Church of Haiti," and at the same time that Church was recognized as an independent part of the Anglican Church. Bishop Holly died in 1911 after serving the Haitian Church with splendid devotion for half a century. Despite his real ability it would have been far better had the Episcopal Church created a missionary district and given the Church adequate supervision during the formative years. It was a case of a Church assuming independence long before it was ready. In the years between Holly's death and 1923, the Episcopal Church gave jurisdiction over Haiti to other missionary bishops, who themselves had all they could do in their own districts. Finally the Church gave Haiti a bishop of its own in the person of Harry R. Carson, former Archdeacon of

Panama. From then onwards the Church began an era of development in spite of the political troubles between 1914 and 1934. During these days a theological school at Port-au-Prince was re-founded, with the result that today most of the clergy are Haitians. Since 1913 the official name of the Church has been "L'Église Orthodoxe Apostolique Haitienne," which adds a further charming note of confusion to the various names of Anglican Churches.

The Dominican Republic comprises the eastern two-thirds of the Island of Haiti and its mountainous terrain is far less productive than the western part of the country. The population, mostly mulatto and Negro, is still largely illiterate, although representative government was established in 1924. The Episcopal Church began work there in 1918, after the West Indian bishops had called attention to the fact that many of their people had migrated to the Dominican Republic. The Reverend William Wyllie went to Santo Domingo City in 1918 and endured great hardship there and received very little support. He later became Archdeacon. At first under the Bishop of Puerto Rico, the jurisdiction was transferred to Haiti in 1918. Now it is a separate missionary district with the Bishop of Haiti in charge.

Puerto Rico and the Virgin Islands. The famous Ponce de Leon became the first of the one hundred forty-two Spanish governors of Puerto Rico in 1509. Discovered by Columbus in 1493, it remained in Spanish hands until 1898, when it was taken over by the United States. Twenty-six years before the latter date a church was organized in Ponce by a clergyman from the Virgin Islands because a number of Anglican West Indians from Antigua had migrated to Puerto Rico and there was no church to care for them. Holy Trinity, Ponce, thus

84

came into being in 1872, the first non-Roman church in the Island.

There was plenty of missionary work to be done, for after four centuries of Spanish rule less than one third of the population could be counted as active Christians. The American Church responded to the need by consecrating a bishop, James H. Van Buren, whose decade of leadership was spent mostly in laying foundations. St. Luke's Hospital, Ponce, was built in 1907 during his episcopate.

Under the next bishop, Charles B. Colmore (1913-47) the Church made great strides, not the least of which was the founding of a seminary at San Juan in 1929, where nationals could be trained for the ministry. In Van Buren's day his small staff was mostly American, whereas today the great majority of the clergy are nationals. Colmore also added a school for nurses at St. Luke's Hospital, and during his time a number of parochial schools were founded. A considerable addition to the strength of the Church came in 1923, when the Reverend Manuel Ferrando, a former Roman Catholic priest, who had built a large independent church and congregation at Quebrada Limon, came over to the Episcopal Church. Ferrando was consecrated suffragan bishop of the District and served in that capacity for a decade. Another interesting development from this Church has been St. Just's Farm School which trains boys in agriculture. Under Bishop Charles F. Boynton (1947-51) there was a further development of parochial schools which augurs well for the Church in the future.

The S.P.G. had done a fair amount of work since 1703 on the three islands that were bought by the United States from Denmark in 1917. As a consequence, when they were transferred from the diocese of Antigua to the American district of Puerto Rico in 1919, there were several good church buildings with which to work. All Saints' Church at St. Thomas had been erected in 1847. The Virgin Islands are a separate missionary district because of the great difference in language and tradition, but the Bishop of Puerto Rico has jurisdiction.

THE MISSIONARY DISTRICTS OF MEXICO; THE CANAL ZONE; AND CENTRAL AMERICA

Mexico. Royal governors from Spain controlled Mexico from the time Cortez overthrew the Aztecs in 1521 until the beginning of the nineteenth century. Resentment at the harshness of Spanish rule brought about a movement for independence in 1810, and fifteen years later the country was declared a republic. There followed several decades of upheaval, but finally in 1857 an Indian leader, Benito Juarez, proclaimed a new constitution with freedom of press and worship, together with a new system of education for the land.

The Episcopal Church was now able to capitalize on three contemporary movements in Mexico. In 1853 a clergyman named Nicholson had formed an independent church called "La Sociedad Catolica Apostolica Mexicana" in the northern part of Mexico. Also some clergy who had withdrawn from the Roman Church, corresponded with an Episcopal priest in New York, the Rev. A. H. DeMora, and together they set up an organization for a reformed church. In addition to these two groups there was a third, lead by a former Dominican friar, Manuel Aguas, who organized "La Iglesia de Jesus" as a successor to Nicholson's church. Nicholson had the support of Churchmen in the United States, and they organized

86

a Mexican Missionary Society and sent the Reverend H. C. Riley to Mexico City.

After some deliberation, the Episcopal Church finally consecrated the Reverend H. C. Riley as Bishop of the Valley of Mexico in 1879, with the result that Mexico now had an organized Episcopal Church. Many subsequent difficulties caused a great decline in the new Church, and it was not until 1904, when Henry D. Aves was consecrated first Missionary Bishop, that the work began to grow; in 1906 "La Iglesia de Jesus" became part of the Missionary District of Mexico under Bishop Aves. There were now only sixty-one congregations and twenty-eight clergy, but Aves gave great leadership and the Church began to grow. Among other wise moves, he took the school for the education of Mexican clergy from Mexico City to Guadalajara, with the result that an increasing number of young men began to fill the ranks of the clergy.

The Revolution of 1911 caused another serious set-back for the Church, for much property was destroyed. Bishop Aves resigned in 1923, and his successor, Frank W. Creighton, was not elected until three years had gone by. These years witnessed increasing control over religion by the government, and many foreign clergy had to leave the country; the Church still had far too few native clergy to do more than hold its own. In 1931 the Archdeacon, Efrain Salinas y Velasco was consecrated suffragan bishop; three years later he became the diocesan. He resigned in 1957 after doing heroic work. The House of Bishops elected José G. Saucedo, a young Mexican priest, as his successor. Today there is a strong work in Mexico City, and the Church in the country areas is growing. Justly famous is the Hooker School for girls in Mexico City.

Panama Canal Zone. In modern times what is now the Canal Zone was part of the Republic of Colombia, until Panama declared its independence in 1903, and "ceded" the Canal Zone to the United States.

Long before this, in 1840, one Matthew Newport persuaded S.P.G. to assist him in his work with the Mosquito Indians, a project which met with great success. The whole area assumed greater importance when the dream of digging a canal began to be realized. By the eighteen-eighties, de Lesseps was trying to pierce the isthmus, and there were some 40,000 West Indians employed on the Canal project, most of whom were Anglicans. In 1907, the Church of England had transferred jurisdiction to the American Church, the Canal was completed in 1914, and five years later the Panama Canal Zone was constituted as an American Missionary District. The Church works amongst the West Indians, with white people who are permanently employed in the area, and with Armed Forces personnel.

A number of further rearrangements of jurisdiction have taken place in recent years, the general effect of which has been to place more responsibility on the American Church. In 1947, the Bishop of Honduras signed over to the Bishop of the Canal Zone the jurisdiction of Nicaragua, Costa Rica, and the northern section of the Republic of Panama. A further change took place in October of 1956, when the Diocese of British Honduras formally relinquished jurisdiction over Guatemala, El Salvador, and Honduras to the American Church.

Central America. As it proved, these steps were preparatory to the establishment of the new missionary jurisdiction of Central America by the American Church in 1956; it comprised

88

Guatemala, Honduras, El Salvador, Nicaragua, and Costa Rica. The latter two countries were taken from the Canal Zone, which now has only Colombia attached to it. The new jurisdiction contains some eight and a half million people many of whom have not had the Gospel preached to them. The first Bishop of this new missionary district is David E. Richards.

THE MISSIONARY DIOCESE
OF ARGENTINA
AND EASTERN SOUTH AMERICA
WITH THE FALKLAND ISLANDS

This huge missionary jurisdiction covers all of South America except Colombia, Venezuela, the diocese of British Guiana, and the southern part of Brazil. The work of the Anglican Church here was in three distinct stages that paralleled the lives of three men: Allen Gardiner in the pioneer stage, Bishop Waite H. Stirling in the founder stage, and Bishop E. F. Every in the era of later organization. These three stages covered a century and more. The story commences with the death by starvation of Commander Allen Gardiner, lately of the Royal Navy, who with his missionary companions died in southern Patagonia after a valiant but fruitless attempt to establish a mission amongst the hostile natives. This was in 1851. He went there under the auspices of the Patagonian Missionary Society which began in 1844, and his object was to establish headquarters in the Falkland Islands, where he proposed to bring likely Patagonian boys from the mainland for Christian training.

Gardiner's successor in the mission was a young clergyman from England, Waite H. Stirling, who arrived at the Falklands in 1863, and immediately carried forward Gardiner's original plan. Stirling met with some success and established a number of missions on the mainland. However, the natives were wanderers by necessity, for food was scarce; and the difficulties of teaching them were well-nigh insuperable. Stirling was called home in 1869 to be consecrated first bishop of the Falkland Islands, with a jurisdiction that covered almost the whole of the Continent. By this time the Patagonian Missionary Society had become the now famous South American Missionary Society (S.A.M.S.), and the Bishop and his helpers developed the work in Patagonia, and opened up missions to the Araucanian Indians and in three regions of the Chaco. Stirling also built a cathedral at Stanley in place of the original cathedral which was destroyed by a landslide.

The South American mission attracted a great deal of attention from the first, due to the dramatic death of Gardiner, the fact that Gardiner's son and grandson worked in the missions, and that Charles Darwin became an ardent supporter of the work when he saw what the Church could accomplish among such primitive, and apparently hopeless, pagans.

Stirling had been bishop for thirty years when he retired, and it was fortunate that he was succeeded by an equally capable man, Bishop E. F. Every, who further developed the work. There were a great many Englishmen with their families in South America in those days, and as a consequence a number of fine churches were built in the coastal cities for their use; and by the turn of the century Buenos Aires had no fewer than seven Church of England congregations, including St. John's, which became the pro-Cathedral in 1910. The collapse of the Chilean nitrate trade, a depression, and two world wars have caused the English population to diminish very considerably, with a resulting lack of support for that part of the work.

A great educational work for underprivileged children was done by an English clergyman, William Case Morris, who devoted himself to this work for many decades in Buenos Aires. By 1932, the year he died, there were twenty-five schools in various parts of the city with a total attendance of more than 71,000 boys and girls.

After being divided into two jurisdictions, the Continent is now embraced by one jurisdiction, and it seems evident that the American Church should be doing much more work in that part of the world. There are still huge areas untouched by any Church, for it is estimated that there are not less than twenty millions of people in South America who are completely unchurched. This is the solid justification for Anglican work in South America.

THE CHURCH IN BRAZIL

The work of the American Church in Brazil actually began at the Virginia Theological Seminary when the American Church Missionary Society sent two young men, Lucien Lee Kinsolving and James W. Morris to begin work at Porto Alegre in 1889. Kinsolving had made his final decision to go to South America while standing at the grave of Bishop Payne in Alexandria. Bishop Payne had been Bishop of Liberia, and on his grave was written, "He gave thirty-three years to the mission field." Earlier attempts to begin Anglican work in Brazil in 1859 and 1866 had petered out, but this new venture took firm root. Bishop Peterkin of Virginia was put in charge of the mission, and when he made a visitation in 1893, he confirmed 142 persons and ordained four deacons. Bishop Stirling likewise paid occasional visits to the mission so that the work was not left entirely unshepherded.

It was obvious, however, that the mission should have a bishop of its own, so they proceeded to elect Kinsolving for the independent "Egreja Episcopal Brasileira" in 1899; eight years later the American Church accepted it as the Missionary District of Southern Brazil. The need for a native ministry was met by founding a theological school at Porto Alegre in 1900, and during the past half-century the school has been instrumental in training a considerable number of Brazilian clergy. Other outstanding institutions are Southern Cross School for boys and girls, also in Porto Alegre, and St. Margaret's School for girls at Pelotas.

By 1950 the single district was divided into three: Central Brazil, Southern Brazil, and Southwestern Brazil. Two out of the three bishops are Brazilian, as are also the great majority of the clergy. A National Council is the central authority for the Church, and although it is not yet a self-governing province, it may well become so not many years hence.

A recent agreement between the Presiding Bishop of the Episcopal Church and the Archbishop of Canterbury did much to clear up the question of jurisdiction in areas where both Churches were at work. The American Church now has control over the entire country of Brazil, and the British churches and chaplaincies there are under the jurisdiction of the Bishop of Central Brazil.

CHAPTER THREE

Africa

Africa

THE CHURCH OF THE PROVINCE OF SOUTH AFRICA

Early in the Christian Era the Faith spread along the northern coast of Africa. The great city of Alexandria will always be associated in the Christian mind with its great teachers, St. Clement, Origen, and St. Athanasius, while St. Cyprian is linked with Carthage, and St. Augustine with Hippo. The early centuries were bright with promise, until the rise of Islam and the Moslem invasion of North Africa in the seventh century, events which practically destroyed the Church in that large area. The Moslems were stopped by the great natural barrier of the Sahara, for it was not until the eleventh century that they began to expand south of the desert. Moslem missionary work was prosecuted here with great vigor in the sixteenth century.

The barrier formed by the Moslem conquest along the northern shore of Africa, the Sahara Desert, and the fact that Africa had few navigable rivers, meant that the great central and southern sections of the continent received little notice from Europe until the latter's steadily growing population, and the search for markets and raw materials turned the eyes of Europe toward the unknown land. The slave trade had been going on for perhaps three hundred years, but those Europeans who were involved in it concerned themselves with the ocean transportation for the slaves, leaving to the Arabs the task of recruiting them from the interior.

Towards the end of the fifteenth century, a Captain Day sailed part of the way down the west coast of Africa; but it was the famous Vasco da Gama who rounded the Cape of Good Hope in 1497 on his way to Calicut on the southwest coast of India. He was followed by others, and it was due to this search for the spice countries that the next attempt to take the Gospel to the interior of Africa was made from the south and the east coasts.

As time went on and trade with the Far East increased, the Cape became a vitally important port of call. It was held by the Dutch who called it "Tavern of the Ocean," until the British took it from them in 1806. This was the beginning of a rivalry between the Dutch and the British in South Africa that has lasted to the present time.

The British treaty with the Dutch stipulated that they would do nothing to interfere with the Dutch Reformed Church at the Cape; in consequence the British did not attempt to evangelize the natives, and indeed they did very little to provide ministrations for their own people who were living at the Cape. When the noted missionary, Henry Martyn, was on his way to India in 1806, he was present at the capture of Capetown, and was asked to officiate at a funeral. He was not able to find a single copy of the Prayer Book in the family of any English resident so, presumably, he either had to rely on his memory or make up a service on the spot.

The founding of the Church Missionary Society in England in 1799 did a great deal to call the attention of the Church of England to its missionary duty and to the needs of South Africa and other lands of the Far East. It was not too soon, for the nineteenth century witnessed a frantic

96

scramble of European nations to stake out claims on the African Continent and elsewhere.

Christian work in South Africa was begun by Moravian missionaries in 1737; much later, in 1798, the London Missionary Society (Congregational) sent a Dr. John Vanderkemp to the Cape where he began work with Hottentots and Kaffirs. The S.P.G. did not send its first missionary to South Africa until 1819, at which time the C.M.S. confined its attention to the west coast. It was a day of small things, for in 1825 there were only six Anglican clergy at the Cape.

Sporadic oversight was given to Anglicans at Capetown by various bishops when their ships stopped on the way to Calcutta and elsewhere. Bishop James was there in 1827, and records that he confirmed some five hundred persons, using the Dutch Reformed Church for the purpose. He also raised more than two thousand pounds for the erection of a church, for which the government had given the land. Two other bishops of Calcutta, Turner and Wilson, each spent a few days at the Cape in 1829 and 1832 respectively, and the latter while he was there confirmed three hundred, consecrated two church sites, and held the first Anglican ordination in South Africa. Bishop Corrie of Madras also visited the colony in 1835, as did Bishop Nixon of Tasmania in 1843.

It became increasingly obvious that such sporadic episcopal oversight was utterly inadequate, and that a bishop must be consecrated for the Cape. It was fortunate that the recently begun Colonial Bishoprics Fund made it possible to endow the bishopric of Capetown and appoint a bishop thereto. The herculean task of beginning organized Anglican work at the Cape fell to Canon Robert Gray of Stockton-on-Tees who was given the choice of a bishopric in Australia or in South

Africa. The thirty-six-year-old cleric chose the Cape, and accordingly he was consecrated on St. Peter's Day, 1847, with three other bishops who were destined for Australia.

This great public service held at Westminster Abbey with a Choral Eucharist and seven hundred sixty communions, was in striking contrast to the hitherto almost secret consecrations of colonial bishops held at Lambeth Palace Chapel. Robert Gray ranks as one of the great Anglican bishops for his work as an ecclesiastical statesman and missionary. He stands with White of the United States, Broughton of Australia, and George A. Selwyn of New Zealand in the former category, while as an indefatigable missionary he had no peer. On his first journey out of Capetown, Gray remarked that he had met with an English Church but that he had had to travel nine hundred miles before coming to it. Very soon after his arrival, Gray began the training of men for Holy Orders and laid plans for missionary work among the natives. The work prospered, for the Bishop's initial clergy group of fourteen in 1847 had grown to more than fifty by 1850.

After eight years of hard work, two new dioceses were erected and bishops appointed for Grahamstown and Natal. Indentured labor came to the latter place begining in 1860 to help in the sugar plantations; they were mostly Hindus, and by 1913 they numbered 115,000. The new diocesan divisions made it necessary for Gray to resign his Letters Patent; but after an interval new Letters were issued to him in 1853. Meanwhile the former Crown Colony was granted representative government, which left some doubt as to the nature and extent of Gray's authority in his own Province. The new Letters Patent were held invalid because no jurisdiction could be given for a colony which had been given responsible government, and where the Church was consequently not established any more. Soon after this no more Letters Patent were issued to colonial bishops, which was a great improvement because it released the growing colonial Churches from the control of the British Government and forced them to set up their own form of Church government based on common agreement.

The unfortunate "Colenso Controversy" came about because of the uncertainty as to Gray's jurisdiction and authority, and the exasperating character of John William Colenso, the Bishop of Natal. Colenso was deposed by Gray for heresy, but he refused to resign on the grounds that when he took the oath of obedience to his metropolitan at his consecration there was no legal metropolitan! As we have seen, Gray had relinquished his Letters Patent before the consecration, and the new ones were not issued until a month after Colenso's consecration and oath. When Gray consecrated Macrorie for Natal, with the title of Pietermaritzburg in 1869, Colenso remained as legal Bishop of Natal since the English courts upheld him. The schism was not healed until 1883. The results of this unhappy affair are still evident, for there is still a so-called "Church of England" in South Africa although its numbers and influence are steadily diminishing. It was now obvious that the method of giving colonial bishops authority by Letters Patent was hopelessly inadequate; the only answer was self-government, and to this end Bishop Gray worked with all his tremendous energy. Autonomy of the Church was brought about through a series of Provincial Synods, beginning with a rather tentative one in 1857 up to the important one of January, 1870. This latter meeting drew up a constitution for the province consisting of twenty-four articles and twenty-seven canons. The Constitution deliberately cut itself off from the Church and civil courts of

99

England, and thus the Church in South Africa became a fully autonomous branch of the Anglican Church. Gray had made it possible for the Church to be free of Whitehall at last.

It was high time for the Church to set her house in order, for there was much to do. As the Church's missionaries moved northward from the Cape they found, in general, three types of natives whom they had to approach: the small Bushmen, wandering hunters who lived in the region nearest the Cape; the Negroes in the upper central and western areas; and the large-framed, intelligent Bantu or Kaffir peoples in the central and eastern sections. Great rivalry existed between the blacks and the whites, and this was true especially of the Boers who lived on the soil and progressively dispossessed the natives. Beginning in the 1830's, the Boers began to migrate north and east of Capetown to the Transvaal and the Orange Free State. Besides an initial dislike for the British they resented the efforts of the various British missions to convert and educate the natives. The Dutch point of view towards the natives was paternalistic, whereas the underlying philosophy of British missionaries, both Anglican and Protestant, looked to eventual liberty and equality for the native peoples.

Congregationalists and Methodists had been working with the natives for some decades before the Anglicans came, but when the latter did begin work, they met with good success. They sometimes created Christian settlements on blocks of land obtained for that purpose; at other times they converted individual natives and encouraged them to stay in their own environment as Christian missionaries. The Anglicans drew no sharp color line, and both blacks and whites attended their synods.

In 1863 the new diocese of the Orange Free State came into being, to be followed in 1870 by Zululand, and in 1873 by

St. John's, Kaffraria. The first bishop of the latter diocese came from the Episcopal Church of Scotland whose special missionary interest has been this area to the present time. By 1891, when Southern Rhodesia became a diocese, Gray's original diocese of Capetown had become eight dioceses, each with a bishop and a growing number of clergy, with church members both white and black.

The British Government tried to annex the Transvaal in 1877 in order to quiet the disorders; they wished this to be the first step in a federation of the Cape, the Orange Free State, and the Transvaal. However, the Boers revolted against the plan, so the Union of South Africa was postponed for a generation.

The rivalry between the British and the Boers culminated in the Boer War when the latter were defeated after a bitter struggle. Finally, when the Union of South Africa was created in 1910, the tension eased somewhat and a new nation that was not a British colony came into being. This era of good will came to an end with the rise of Afrikander nationalism after World War I, and since that time the government, aided by the Dutch Reformed Church, has become progressively more fixed in its determination to keep the colored and native populations in complete subjection. Most Dutch Reformed churchmen cling to the idea that the African is a member of a permanently inferior race, so that complete segregation and subjugation are the only right answers. Out of a total population of twelve million, there are but two and a half million whites; three-fifths of these speak Afrikaans and two-fifths speak English. There are eight million natives, one million colored (mixed ancestry), and a quarter of a million Indians who live mostly in Natal.

The natives and colored people have no political, social,

or educational rights, and they are subjected to all types of indignities and compelled to live in the worst kind of slums. Hundreds of thousands of natives, uprooted from tribal life, work in the gold and diamond mines for years on end without family life. Crime and violence are understandably rampant, and these are dealt with by stern and often brutal repression by the government. In 1948, the predominantly white Afrikaans voters overturned the long dominant United Party of Jan Christiaan Smuts, and proceeded to institute a rigid policy of "apartheid" whereby every nonwhite—whether black, colored, Asiatic, or half-caste—must live apart from the whites except in a servant-master relationship. The recent Native Laws Amendment Bill seeks further to restrict not only the social life but the public worship of non-whites by giving the Minister of Native Affairs the power to determine who shall worship in a particular church. The reaction of the leaders of the Church has been sharp and courageous: The Cathedral of St. George in Capetown states on its outside notice board that all of the services are open to all people at all times; and the bishops of the Province have served notice to the government that if the proposed Amendment becomes law they will not be able to obey it and that they will counsel their clergy and lay people to disobey it.

The situation is particularly grave in the city of Johannesburg, which is in the center of the Gold Reef discovered in 1886. The Church has notable missions at Sophiatown operated by the Wantage Sisters and the Fathers of the Community of the Resurrection; and at Rosettenville, the headquarters of the latter Community. The principal theological college for Africans in the Province is at Rosettenville, and there is also a school for boys and girls. These missions are threatened by a new government proposal to move all the natives to another location without compensation to them or to the Church.

The Church has not lacked great and prophetic voices in Bishop Ambrose Reeves of Johannesburg; Fr. Trevor Huddleston and Fr. Raynes of the Community of the Resurrection; Fr. Michael Scott, a priest who has worked for years in southwest Africa among the Herreros; and Alan Paton, who has written two novels on South Africa: *Cry, The Beloved Country* and *Too Late the Phalarope*.

The Church of the Province consists of fourteen dioceses covering a larger area than the Union of South Africa, for in it is included Damaraland, the former German Southwest Africa, and Lebombo in Portuguese East Africa. There are a hundred churches in this latter diocese where the clergy use Portuguese as well as six African dialects for their services. The Provincial Synod meets every five years, and in it the clergy and delegates of the various races meet together on terms of complete equality. Anglicans are the second largest body of Christians in the Union, with the Dutch Reformed Church in first place. Bishops are elected by clergy and laity of the diocese, but if they fail to reach a decision they may request the metropolitan to consult with the Archbishop of Canterbury and choose a bishop from the Church of England.

Prayer Book revision has had its place in the life of the Church, for the first Liturgical Committee was formed in 1908. The Provincial Synod of 1924 gave its approval to an alternative Liturgy for the Holy Communion, and twelve years later it approved the alternative Kalendar and Occasional Offices. By 1950 it endorsed the revision of the Book of Common Prayer which latter made its appearance in 1954. In general the revision follows "1549" rather than

"1552" or "1662," in which respect it is similar to the Scottish and American Prayer Books.

Religious Communities have been prominent in the life of the Church almost from the beginning, when Bishop Gray brought eight ladies from England in 1868 to form a kind of sisterhood. Nearly every diocese has a Community working in it today, and in some cases more than one, there being three Communities for men and eight for women. The Church's role in education has been a notable one both among the innumerable mission schools and in the outstanding boys' and girls' schools in many dioceses.

The Church of the Province of South Africa, with more than a million members, is a little more than a century old and it has come through many troubles. The number of blacks and colored who belong to it is increasing; its leaders are courageous, and although the testing of the present time is severe, and will doubtless grow more so, the Church is nevertheless witnessing to her Faith with prophetic insight and fearlessness.

In quaint and startling contrast to the mainland dioceses is the lonely island of Tristan da Cunha, a part of the diocese of St. Helena. Tristan lies 1,320 miles south southwest from the latter island, and all but seven of its population of 300 are Anglicans. S.P.G. first sent a full-time priest there in 1851, and there has continued to be a resident priest there up to the present time.

THE PROVINCE OF CENTRAL AFRICA

There are at present eleven dioceses in Central and Eastern Tropical Africa, seven of which do not as yet belong to a Province but are under the metropolitical jurisdiction of the Archbishop of Canterbury. The four southernmost

104

dioceses in this group of eleven, Northern Rhodesia, Matabeleland, Mashonaland, and Nyasaland, form the Province of Central Africa. In order to form the province, which is coterminous with the new political Federation of 1953, the Archbishop of Capetown resigned jurisdiction of Southern Rhodesia which was made into two dioceses, Mashonaland and Matabeleland; and the Archbishop of Canterbury resigned jurisdiction of Northern Rhodesia and Nyasaland. The Federation of Central Africa was a deliberate plan on the part of the British Government to alleviate the tension between the races and to prevent Southern Rhodesia from gravitation into the orbit of South Africa.

It was on May 8, 1955, lacking two years of a century since Livingstone had made his famous appeal for missionaries to Central Africa, that the Archbishop of Canterbury, Dr. Fisher, inaugurated the new province at the Cathedral at Salisbury in the presence of more than two thousand people of all races "from the Governor-General and the Federal Prime Minister to African women with babies on their backs." [14] Almost half the clergy were Africans. The Province elected the Bishop of Mashonaland, Dr. Paget, as the first Archbishop. Of prime importance is the Theological College at Lusaka which will continue to train Africans for the ministry. The northern part of the Province, Northern Rhodesia, was originally under the care of the Universities Mission to Central Africa, while the southern part, taken from the Province of South Africa, has a strong S.P.G. background.

THE MISSIONARY DIOCESES
OF EAST AFRICA

Two of these dioceses, Zanzibar and Masasi, cover the original area of the Universities Mission to Central

Africa, while the five remaining ones, Central Tanganyika, Southwest Tanganyika, Mombasa, Upper Nile and Uganda are largely the spiritual children of C.M.S. For convenience the first two dioceses may be called East Africa while the area contained by the five dioceses may be called Eastern Equatorial Africa.

East Africa. By the middle of the nineteenth century it was clear that if Christian missionaries were to penetrate the central hinterland of Africa, they must do so from the south and east coasts and not from the west. C.M.S. did pioneer work on the eastern coast, and it was one of their missionaries, Johann Krapf, who conceived a sound strategy for planting the Church in the interior. He reasoned that the Church, beginning on the mainland opposite Zanzibar, would establish a string of missions each one farther westward. Krapf arrived in Zanzibar in 1844 and he and his partner, Jacob Rebmann, started a mission on the mainland at Rabai two years later. This was an important period for David Livingstone was to cross the continent from east to west in 1849, while in the next decade the explorations of Burton, Speke, and others added to the excited interest of westerners in the "Dark Continent."

Bishop George Augustus Selwyn had delivered a series of sermons at Cambridge in 1854, and these had greatly stimulated the University's interest in Christian missions. So, when David Livingstone, recently returned from Africa, made his stirring missionary appeal at Cambridge in 1857, there resulted the formation of the Universities' Mission to Central Africa (U.M.C.A). At first only Oxford and Cambridge were involved, but shortly thereafter Durham and Dublin were included. Charles Frederick Mackenzie was consecrated at

St. Columba at Iona
563

St. Aidan at
Holy Isle of
Lindisfarne
635

Coming of Danes

PROVINCE
OF
YORK

York Minster

CHURCH
IN
WALES

St. David's Cathedral

ST. DAVID'S

St. Woolo's Cathedral
MONMOUTH

PROVINCE OF CANTERBURY

Canterbury Cathedral

Llandaff Cathedral

St. Augustine
597

William of Normandy
1066

Spanish Armada

ENGLAND AND WALES

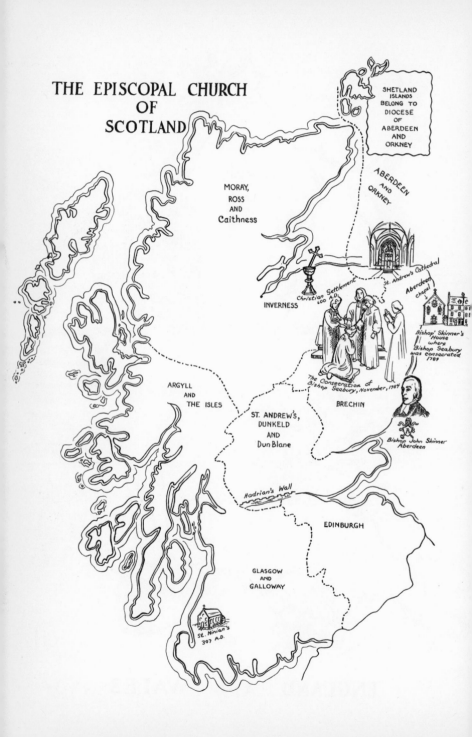

THE EPISCOPAL CHURCH
OF
SCOTLAND

SHETLAND
ISLANDS
BELONG TO
DIOCESE
OF
ABERDEEN
AND
ORKNEY

ABERDEEN
AND
ORKNEY

MORAY,
ROSS
AND
Caithness

St. Andrew's Cathedral

Aberdeen
Chapel

INVERNESS

Christian Settlement 400 A.D.

Bishop' Skinner's
House
where
Bishop Seabury
was consecrated
1784

The Consecration of
Bishop Seabury, November, 1784

ARGYLL
AND
THE ISLES

ST. ANDREW'S,
DUNKELD
AND
Dun Blane

BRECHIN

Bishop John Skinner
Aberdeen

Hadrian's Wall

EDINBURGH

GLASGOW
AND
GALLOWAY

St. Ninian's
397 A.D.

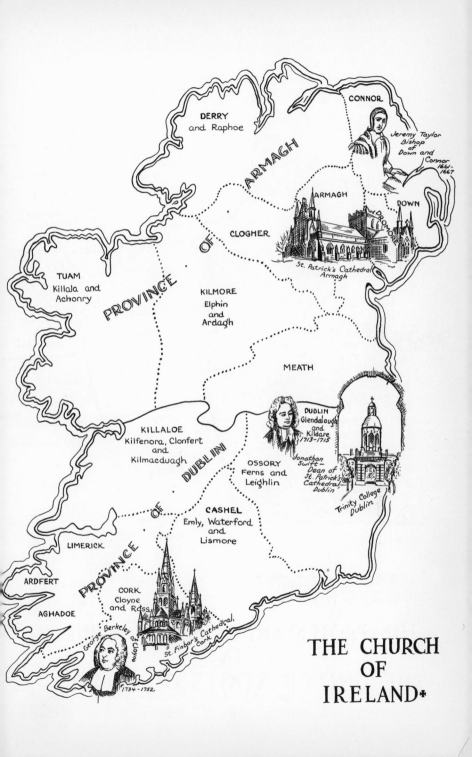

DERRY
and Raphoe

CONNOR

Jeremy Taylor
Bishop
of
Down and
Connor
1661-
1667

PROVINCE OF ARMAGH

ARMAGH

CLOGHER

DOWN

DROMORE

St. Patrick's Cathedral
Armagh

TUAM
Killala and
Achonry

KILMORE
Elphin
and
Ardagh

MEATH

DUBLIN
Glendalough
and
Kildare
1713-1715

KILLALOE
Kilfenora, Clonfert
and
Kilmacduagh

OSSORY
Ferns and
Leighlin

Jonathan
Swift —
Dean of
St. Patrick's
Cathedral
Dublin

Trinity College
Dublin

PROVINCE OF DUBLIN

CASHEL
Emly, Waterford
and
Lismore

LIMERICK

ARDFERT

AGHADOE

CORK
Cloyne
and Ross

George Berkeley of Cloyne

St. Finbar's Cathedral,
Cork

1734 - 1752

THE CHURCH
OF
IRELAND✠

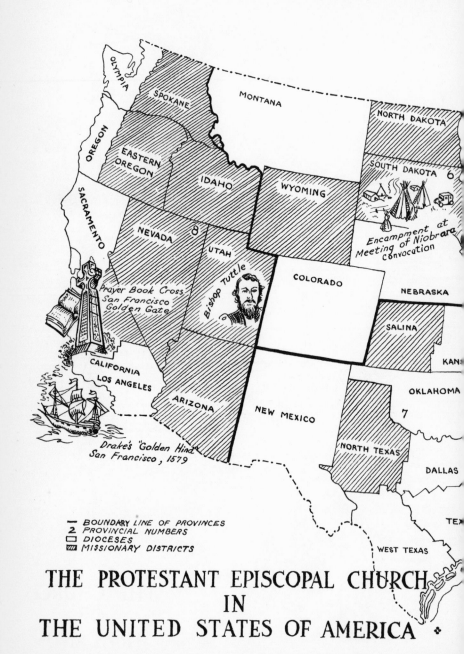

OLYMPIA
OREGON
SPOKANE
MONTANA
NORTH DAKOTA
EASTERN OREGON
IDAHO
WYOMING
SOUTH DAKOTA 6
SACRAMENTO
NEVADA
8
UTAH
COLORADO
NEBRASKA
Encampment at Meeting of Niobrara Convocation
Bishop Tuttle
Prayer Book Cross San Francisco Golden Gate
SALINA
KANS
CALIFORNIA
LOS ANGELES
ARIZONA
NEW MEXICO
OKLAHOMA
7
Drake's "Golden Hind" San Francisco, 1579
NORTH TEXAS
DALLAS
TEX
— BOUNDARY LINE OF PROVINCES
2 PROVINCIAL NUMBERS
☐ DIOCESES
▨ MISSIONARY DISTRICTS
WEST TEXAS

THE PROTESTANT EPISCOPAL CHURCH
IN
THE UNITED STATES OF AMERICA

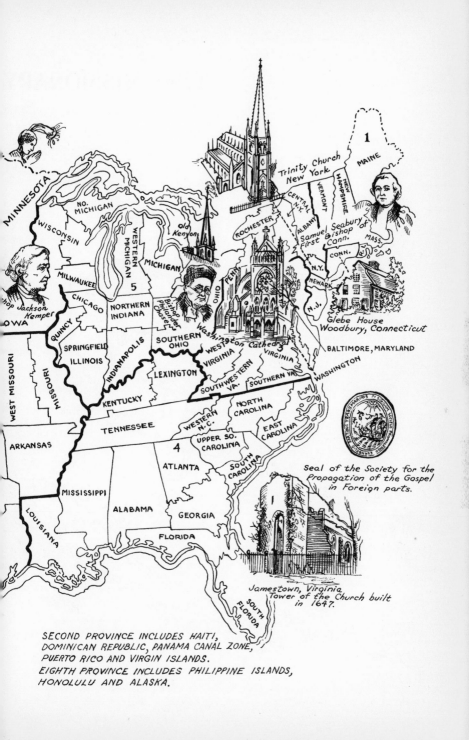

MINNESOTA

WISCONSIN

NO. MICHIGAN

WESTERN MICHIGAN

MICHIGAN

MILWAUKEE

CHICAGO

Bishop Jackson Kemper

IOWA

QUINCY

SPRINGFIELD

ILLINOIS

WEST MISSOURI

MISSOURI

ARKANSAS

LOUISIANA

MISSISSIPPI

ALABAMA

NORTHERN INDIANA

INDIANAPOLIS

KENTUCKY

TENNESSEE

5

SOUTHERN OHIO

OHIO

PENN.

LEXINGTON

WESTERN N.C.

UPPER SO. CAROLINA

4

ATLANTA

GEORGIA

FLORIDA

SOUTH FLORIDA

SOUTH CAROLINA

Old Kenyon

Bishop Philander Chase

Washington Cathedral

VIRGINIA

SOUTHWESTERN VA.

SOUTHERN VA.

WEST VIRGINIA

NORTH CAROLINA

EAST CAROLINA

ROCHESTER

CENTRAL N.Y.

ALBANY

Samuel Seabury First Bishop of Conn.

N.Y.

NEWARK

N.J.

WASHINGTON

VERMONT

NEW HAMPSHIRE

MAINE

1

CONN.

MASS.

Trinity Church New York

Glebe House Woodbury, Connecticut

BALTIMORE, MARYLAND

Seal of the Society for the Propagation of the Gospel in Foreign parts.

Jamestown, Virginia Tower of the Church built in 1647.

SECOND PROVINCE INCLUDES HAITI, DOMINICAN REPUBLIC, PANAMA CANAL ZONE, PUERTO RICO AND VIRGIN ISLANDS.
EIGHTH PROVINCE INCLUDES PHILIPPINE ISLANDS, HONOLULU AND ALASKA.

THE MISSIONARY

Legend

Missions ✚
Outstations ○

PT. LAY

✚ PT. HOPE

○

KOTZEBUE

Typical church

St. John
in the
Wilderness

HUGHES ○

CUT OFF
VILLAGE

ALLAKAK

COSCHAK

NORTON SOUND

HOLOGOCHAKET

ANVIK ✚
BONAZILA ○

○ SHAGELUK

DISTRICT OF ALASKA

CANADA

ARCTIC CIRCLE

...STIAN

ARCTIC VILLAGE
VILLAGE
CHALKITSIK
SALMON
VENETIE
BEAVER
STEVENS
VILLAGE
FORT
YUKON
CIRCLE
Hudson Stuck Memorial
Hospital

RAMPART
SPRINGS
MINTO
FAIRBANKS
NENANA
HEALY
LAKE
Mt. Mckinley

EAGLE

Missionaries traveled Yukon to Anvik.

MANSFIELD
TANACROSS
TETLIN
NABESNA VILLAGE
NORTHWAY

ALASKA HIGHWAY

Holy Trinity
Church
Pro-Cathedral

JUNEAU

VALDEZ
CORDOVA
Mt.
St. Elias

EWARD

DOUGLAS

SITKA

PETERSBURG
WRANGEL

KETCHIKAN

Bishop Peter T. Rowe

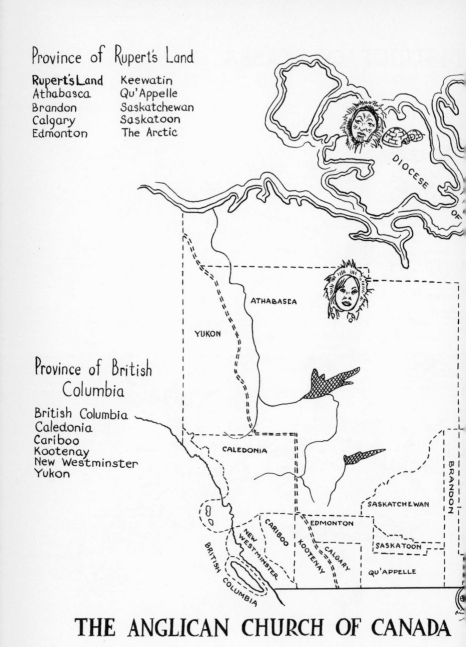

Province of Rupert's Land

Rupert's Land · Keewatin
Athabasca · Qu'Appelle
Brandon · Saskatchewan
Calgary · Saskatoon
Edmonton · The Arctic

Province of British
Columbia

British Columbia
Caledonia
Cariboo
Kootenay
New Westminster
Yukon

THE ANGLICAN CHURCH OF CANADA

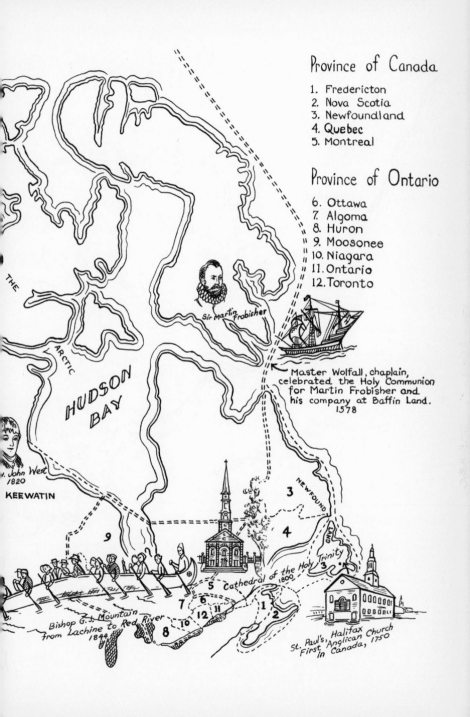

Province of Canada

1. Fredericton
2. Nova Scotia
3. Newfoundland
4. Quebec
5. Montreal

Province of Ontario

6. Ottawa
7. Algoma
8. Huron
9. Moosonee
10. Niagara
11. Ontario
12. Toronto

Sir Martin Frobisher

Master Wolfall, chaplain, celebrated the Holy Communion for Martin Frobisher and his company at Baffin Land. 1578

THE

ARCTIC

HUDSON BAY

John West 1820

KEEWATIN

NEWFOUND LAND

Cathedral of the Holy Trinity 1800

Holy Trinity

Bishop G. J. Mountain from Lachine to Red River 1844

St. Paul's, Halifax First Anglican Church in Canada, 1750

MISSIONARY DISTRICT OF THE
CANAL ZONE.

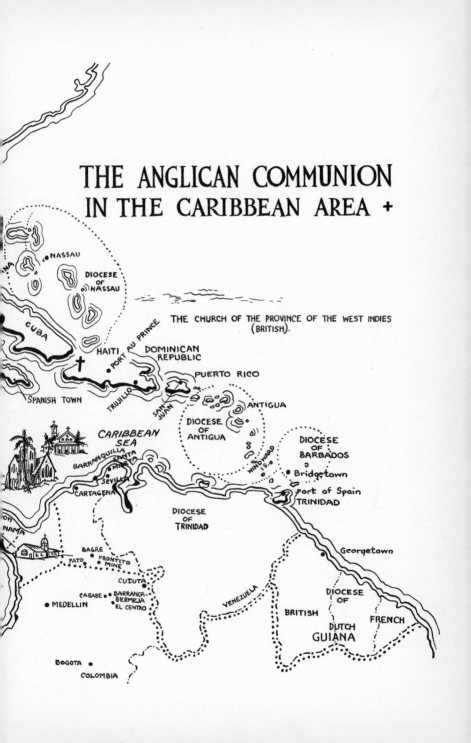

THE ANGLICAN COMMUNION
IN THE CARIBBEAN AREA +

NASSAU

DIOCESE OF NASSAU

CUBA

THE CHURCH OF THE PROVINCE OF THE WEST INDIES (BRITISH).

HAITI PORT AU PRINCE DOMINICAN REPUBLIC

PUERTO RICO

SPANISH TOWN

TRUJILLO

SAN JUAN

ANTIGUA

DIOCESE OF ANTIGUA

CARIBBEAN SEA

BARRANQUILLA SANTA MARTA

SEVILLA

CARTAGENA

WINDWARD IS.

DIOCESE OF BARBADOS

Bridgetown

Port of Spain TRINIDAD

DIOCESE OF TRINIDAD

NAMA

BAGRE

PATO FRONTITO MINE

CUCUTA

CASABE BARRANCA-BERMEJA
MEDELLIN EL CENTRO

VENEZUELA

Georgetown

DIOCESE OF

BRITISH

DUTCH FRENCH

GUIANA

BOGOTA
COLOMBIA

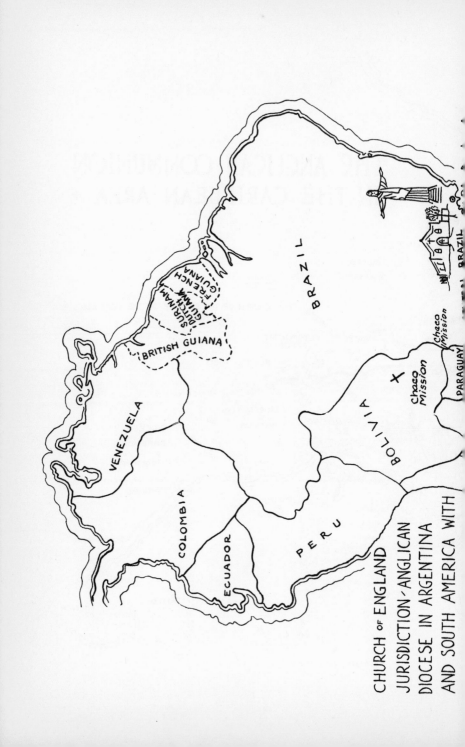

CHURCH of ENGLAND
JURISDICTION - ANGLICAN
DIOCESE IN ARGENTINA
AND SOUTH AMERICA WITH

THE EPISCOPAL CHURCH
IN
SOUTH AMERICA

under American Church.

Argentina, N.Brazil, Uruguay,
Paraguay, Chile, Peru, Ecuador,
Bolivia with the Falkland
Islands.

Argentine
Chaco
Mission

ARGENTINA

BRAZIL

URUGUAY

CHILE

PATAGONIA

Araucanian
Missions

CAPTAIN
ALLEN
FRANCIS
GARDINER
1794~1851
Gave name of Berea
to first Christian settlement

Place of
death

FALKLAND~ISLANDS

St. David's
Chubut

Stanley Cathedral

The Yawl "Allen Gardiner"

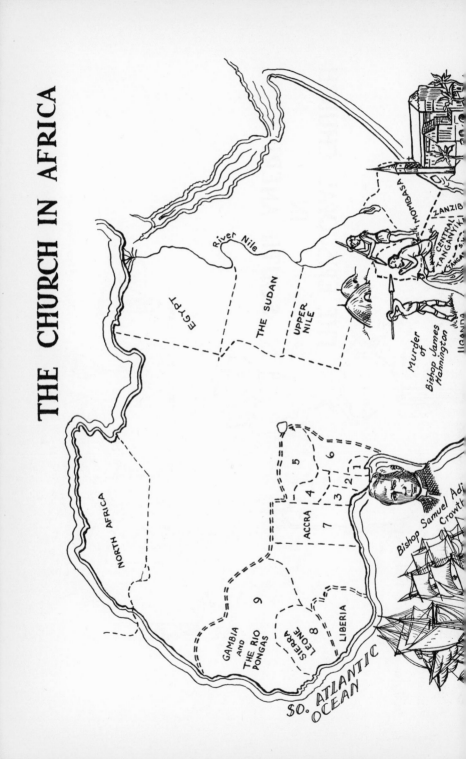

THE CHURCH IN AFRICA

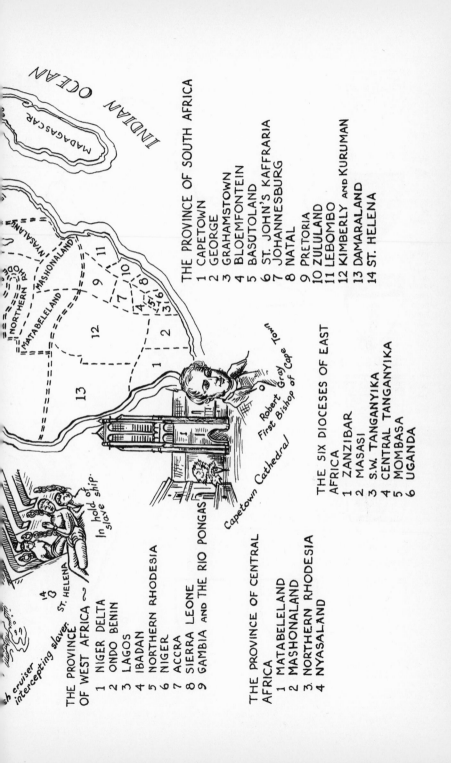

INDIAN OCEAN

MADAGASCAR

THE PROVINCE OF SOUTH AFRICA
1 CAPETOWN
2 GEORGE
3 GRAHAMSTOWN
4 BLOEMFONTEIN
5 BASUTOLAND
6 ST. JOHN'S KAFFRARIA
7 JOHANNESBURG
8 NATAL
9 PRETORIA
10 ZULULAND
11 LEBOMBO
12 KIMBERLY AND KURUMAN
13 DAMARALAND
14 ST. HELENA

Robert Gray
First Bishop of Cape
Capetown Cathedral

THE SIX DIOCESES OF EAST
AFRICA
1 ZANZIBAR
2 MASASI
3 S.W. TANGANYIKA
4 CENTRAL TANGANYIKA
5 MOMBASA
6 UGANDA

sh cruiser
intercepting slaver.
ST. HELENA
In hold of
slave ship

THE PROVINCE
OF WEST AFRICA
1 NIGER DELTA
2 ONDO BENIN
3 LAGOS
4 IBADAN
5 NORTHERN RHODESIA
6 NIGER
7 ACCRA
8 SIERRA LEONE
9 GAMBIA AND THE RIO PONGAS

THE PROVINCE OF CENTRAL
AFRICA
1 MATABELELAND
2 MASHONALAND
3 NORTHERN RHODESIA
4 NYASALAND

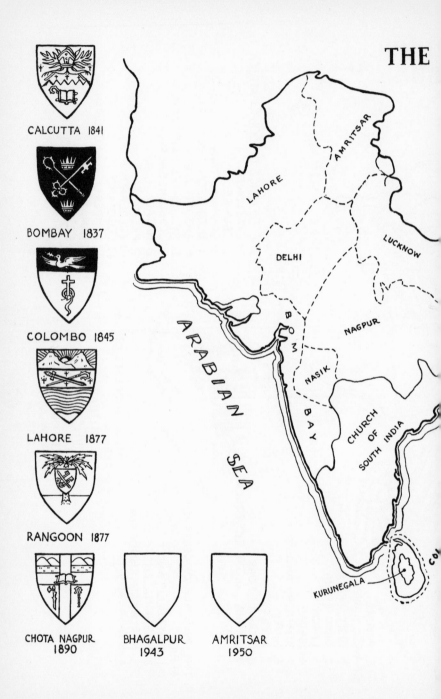

CALCUTTA 1841

BOMBAY 1837

COLOMBO 1845

LAHORE 1877

RANGOON 1877

CHOTA NAGPUR 1890

BHAGALPUR 1943

AMRITSAR 1950

THE

LAHORE

AMRITSAR

DELHI

LUCKNOW

NAGPUR

NASIK

CHURCH OF SOUTH INDIA

ARABIAN SEA

B O M B A Y

KURUNEGALA

Col

CHURCH OF INDIA, PAKISTAN, BURMA AND CEYLON

LUCKNOW 1893

NAGPUR 1902

ASSAM 1915

NASIK 1929

KURUNEGALA 1950

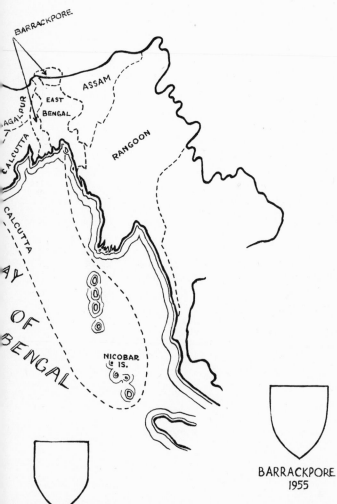

BARRACKPORE 1955

DELHI 1947

EAST BENGAL 1955

THE CHURCH OF ENGLAND
IN
AUSTRALIA AND TASMANIA+

NORTHWEST AUSTRALIA

PROVINCE OF WEST AUSTRALIA

PERTH

KALGOORLIE

BUNBURY

DIOCESES NOT INCLUDED IN A PROVINCE-
ADELAIDE 1
TASMANIA 2
WILLOCHRA 3

PROVINCE
OF
VICTORIA

4 MELBOURNE	7 GIPPSLAND
5. BALLARAT	8 BENDIGO
6. WANGARATTA	9 ST. ARNAUD

ARPENTARIA

PROVINCE OF

QUEENSLAND

NORTH QUEENSLAND

ROCKHAMPTON

Australian Bushman

BRISBANE

WILLOCHRA

3

PROVINCE OF

NEW SOUTH WALES

ARMIDALE

GRAFTON

NEW CASTLE

BATHURST

SYDNEY

Bishop William Grant Broughton

ADELAIDE

1

RIVERINA

CANBERRA AND GOULBURN

9

8

PROVINCE OF

OF

VICTORIA

6

5

4

7

St. Andrew's Cathedral

2

+THE CHURCH
OF THE PROVINCE
OF
NEW ZEALAND

AUCKLAND

BAY OF ISLANDS

Mariner's Cross

WAIKATO

WELLINGTON

WAIAPU

Maori chief

CAPE FAREWELL

"Lone wooden cross"

NELSON

George Augustus Selwyn
Bishop of New Zealand

CHRISTCHURCH

DUNEDIN

Christchurch Cathedral

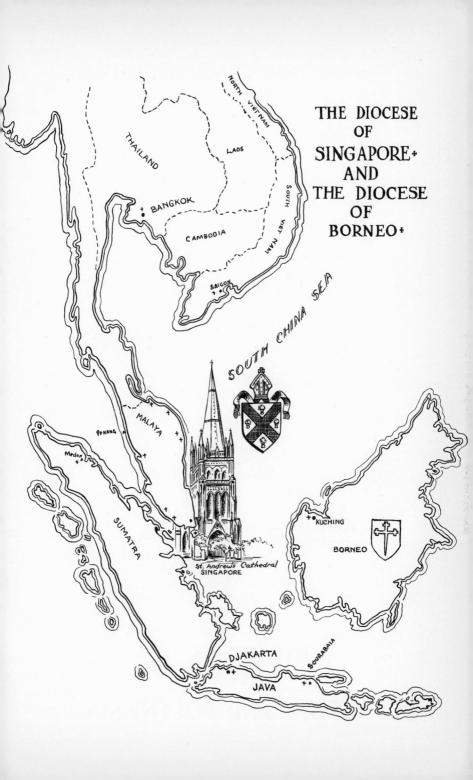

THE DIOCESE
OF
SINGAPORE +
AND
THE DIOCESE
OF
BORNEO +

THAILAND

NORTH VIET NAM

LAOS

+ BANGKOK

CAMBODIA

SOUTH VIET NAM

SAIGON

SOUTH CHINA SEA

MALAYA

PENANG

Medan

SUMATRA

KUCHING

BORNEO

St. Andrews Cathedral
SINGAPORE

DJAKARTA

SOURABAIA

JAVA

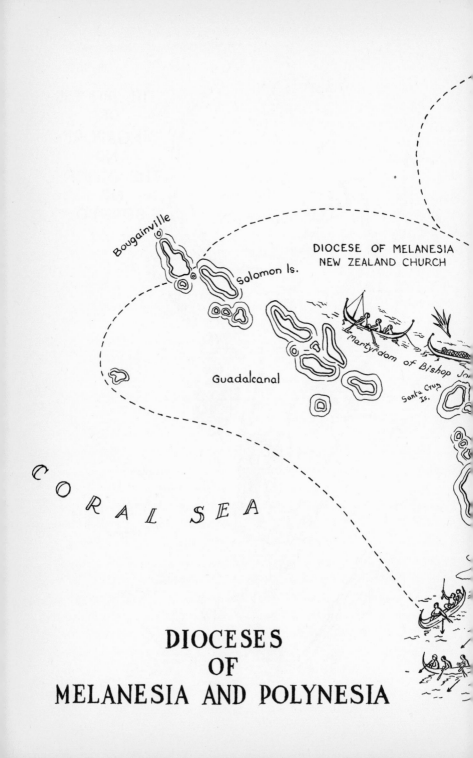

Bougainville

Solomon Is.

DIOCESE OF MELANESIA
NEW ZEALAND CHURCH

Guadalcanal

Martyrdom of Bishop Jn.

Santa Cruz Is.

C O R A L   S E A

DIOCESES
OF
MELANESIA AND POLYNESIA

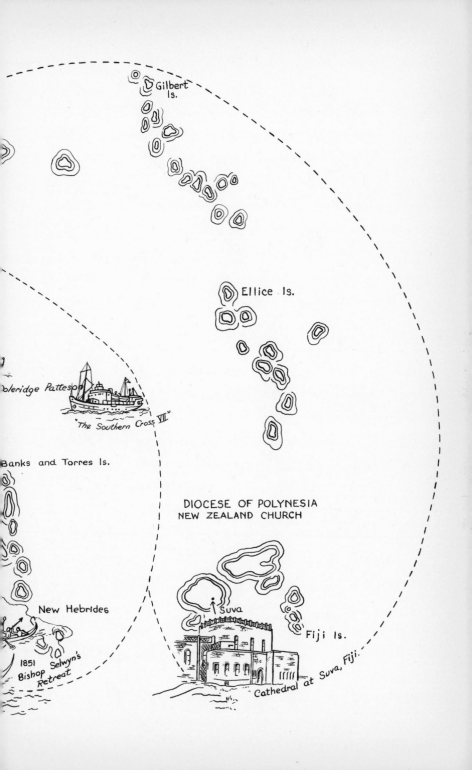

Gilbert Is.

Ellice Is.

oleridge Patteson

"The Southern Cross VII"

Banks and Torres Is.

DIOCESE OF POLYNESIA
NEW ZEALAND CHURCH

Suva

Fiji Is.

New Hebrides

1851 Selwyn's
Bishop Retreat

Cathedral at Suva, Fiji.

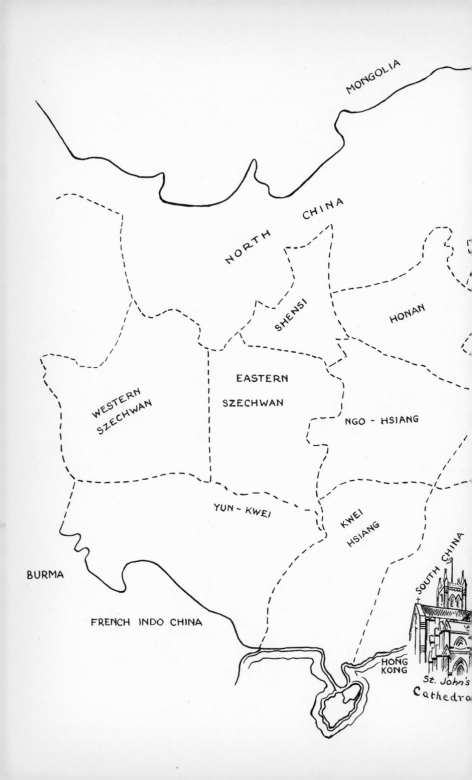

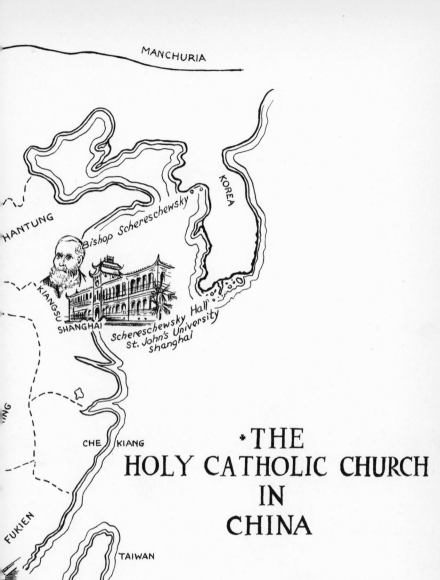

MANCHURIA

KOREA

HANTUNG

Bishop Schereschewsky

KIANGSU

SHANGHAI

Schereschewsky Hall
St. John's University
shanghai

CHE KIANG

FUKIEN

TAIWAN

·THE
HOLY CATHOLIC CHURCH
IN
CHINA

CHUNG HUA SHENG KUNG HUI

THE PHILIPPINE EPISCOPAL CHURCH

SEAL OF THE MISSIONARY DISTRICT OF THE PHILIPPINE ISLANDS

PACIFIC OCEAN

SAMAR

Hospital of St. Theodore's

TABUK

BALBALASANG

BESAO
BONTOC
SAGADA
TAPIAN
BAGNEN

Brent School
Easter School

Holy Trinity Cathedral
St. Andrew's Theological Seminary

St. Luke's Hospital

MANILA
Bishop Brent

LON-OY
TRINIDAD
BAGUIO →

Convent and Girls' School Church of St. Mary the Virgin

LUZON

MINDORO

SIBUYAN SEA

Valid Episcopacy
Given Philippine Church
April 7, 1948

CHINA

MINDANAO

LEYTE

BOHOL

MINDANAO SEA

CEBU

NEGROS

PANAY

SULU SEA

PALAWAN

AWANG
LIBUNGAN
UPI
HALKAN
St. Francis of Assisi

Brent Hospital

Good Shepherd's School

ZAMBOANGA

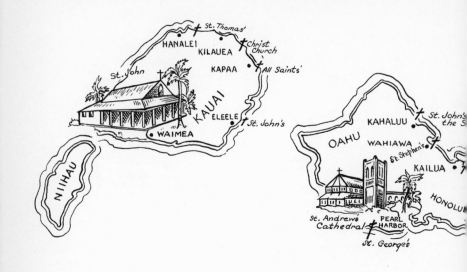

THE
CHURCH
IN THE
HAWAIIAN ISLANDS

THE MISSIONARY DISTRICT OF

istopher

MOLOKAI

Grace Church ✝

✝ Good Shepherd

WAILUKU ●

LANAI

● LAHAINA
Holy ✝
Innocents

MAUI

KAHOOLAWE

KULA ●
✝ St. John's

KOHALA ● ✝ St. Augustine's

KAMUELA ● ✝ St. James'

HONOKAA ●
✝ St. Columba's

PAAUILO ●
OOKALA ●

PAPAALOA ●
✝ St. James'

Kamehameha's
Statue

HILO ●

HAWAII

Cook's KONA
Monument ●

Church of the
Holy
Apostles

KEALAKEKUA ●

✝ Christ
Church

Kilauea
Crater

Captain Cook
discovered Island
in 1778

HONOLULU

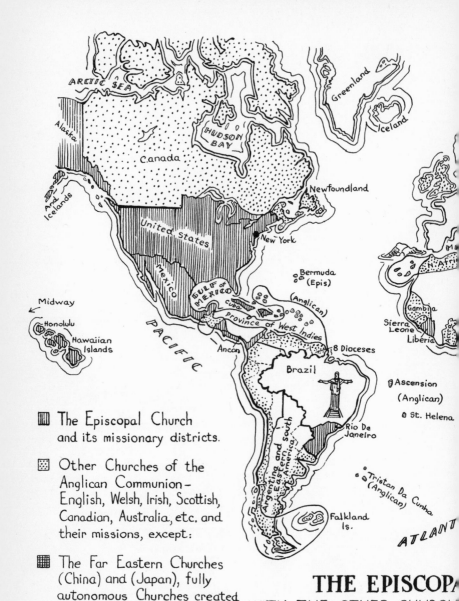

The Episcopal Church and its missionary districts.

Other Churches of the Anglican Communion – English, Welsh, Irish, Scottish, Canadian, Australia, etc. and their missions, except:

The Far Eastern Churches (China) and (Japan), fully autonomous Churches created through missionary efforts of Churches in the United States, England, and Canada.

THE EPISCOPA
WITH THE OTHER CHURCH

CHURCH AROUND THE WORLD
AND MISSIONS OF THE ANGLICAN COMMUNION

THE CHURCH OF JAPAN
NIPPON SEI KO KWAI

HOKKAIDO

Sapporo
Hakodate

Aomori

Hirosaki

Akita

SEA OF JAPAN

TOHOKU

Yamagata

Wakamatso

Koriyama

Toyama

NORTH KANTO
Nikko

Kanazawa

Takasaki

Mito

St. Luke's Hospital
Tokyo

Omiya

Tokyo

St. Paul's
University

Yokohama

MID-JAPAN

Nagoya

SOUTH TOKYO

Kyoto

KYOTO

Kobe

Osaka

KOBE

Hiroshima

Tokushima

OSAKA

Wakayama

Shimonoseki

KOBE

PACIFIC OCEAN

Fukuoka

Kumamoto

KYUSHU

Capetown to work with "the tribes dwelling in the neighbourhood of Lake Nyasa and River Shiré." No stranger to Africa, Mackenzie had been a missionary in Natal; so he entered into his new work with zeal and high hopes, for Livingstone himself accompanied Mackenzie and his staff to the Zambesi and chose the site for the original mission. The missionaries, however, had no idea how bad the local situation was, for the slave trading and the tribal wars caused great havoc. And in addition to these troubles Mackenzie had to use force to free slaves. The Bishop died of malaria on the last day of 1862, only a year after his consecration, and his successor, William George Tozer, wisely decided to give up work in the interior for the moment and take the mission headquarters to Zanzibar. In the latter center he felt he could begin the training of native teachers and more effectively oppose the slave trade, which had its center there.

By a treaty with Britain in 1873 the Sultan agreed that no more slaves would be brought from overseas, so at long last Zanzibar's great slave market was closed. Bishop Tozer resigned in that same year after laying solid foundations for his brilliant successor, Edward Steere, who took full advantage of the opportunities. Steere, who had come out with Tozer in 1863, was a lawyer, a theologian, a linguist, and an architect, as well as being an able and consecrated missionary bishop. Since Swahili was the *lingua franca* of the area, Steere wrote an immensely helpful Swahili grammar, and also began a translation of the Bible into the same language. Steere also accepted the suggestion of one of his clergy, the Reverend A. N. West, and bought the former slave market site for the projected cathedral which the Bishop himself designed and built. The altar stands at the exact place where the whipping

107

post once stood; and that particular piece of ground was given by a Hindu merchant, Javiam Senji. Steere died in 1882 and very fittingly he was buried behind the Cathedral's high altar.

Neither did Steere confine his attention to Zanzibar, for work started again on the mainland before his death. In 1881 two clergymen, W. P. Johnson and Charles Janson got to Lake Nyasa, the original object of the mission, although Janson died upon his arrival there. Johnson saw the possibilities of the area; and when he visited Likoma, an island on the lake, he determined that a small steamer would be the ideal way to bring the Gospel to the people in the villages by the lake side. Accordingly, a twenty-five ton steamer was built in England, then taken apart and shipped in sixty-pound packages to the upper Zambesi where it was assembled; it reached Likoma in 1886 and was called the *Charles Janson*. Work was begun at Likoma and a site was purchased for a mission where in former years people had been burned for witchcraft. This is the site of the present Cathedral. With Likoma as a center and the boat for a conveyance missionary work spread around the lake.

Charles Alan Smythies, who succeeded Steere in 1883, was the last bishop of the undivided area. He had to work under great handicaps, for in 1887 a treaty between England, France, and Germany caused all the mainland work of the mission to go under the German flag. It is interesting that one of Smythies' traveling companions in the early days of his episcopate was Abdullah Susi, one of the two men who carried Livingstone's body to the coast; it was after this experience that Abdullah became a Christian.

By 1892 Nyasaland was set off as a separate diocese, but its first two bishops lasted only three years. Bishop Hornby resigned due to ill-health after two years, and his successor, Chauncy Maples, was drowned in Lake Nyasa in 1895, three months after his consecration. In spite of these handicaps the work went forward, aided by the fact that in 1907 Central Africa became the British Nyasaland Protectorate. Perhaps the most colorful leader of this period is Frank Weston, fourth Bishop of Zanzibar (1908-1924), who had been in the diocese for some years before his consecration. His diocese was particularly hard hit by World War I, for all of the mainland work was in German territory and the missionaries were interned for the duration of the war; the native teachers and clergy were also very badly treated by the Germans. It took a long time to get the work started again in 1918. Weston was a striking person, who spoke his mind fearlessly, as he did notably, when Anglicans and Free Churchmen at Kikuyu planned on cooperative measures that countered Catholic principles. He likewise greatly impressed the Lambeth Conference of 1922 with his forthright sincerity and missionary zeal.

The original diocese became two in 1892, and became three in 1907 when Northern Rhodesia was separated. It is interesting that the latter had as its first diocesan the Right Reverend J. E. Hine, who had been in Africa since 1888. In succession he was priest and doctor in Nyasaland, Bishop of Likoma (Nyasaland) for five years, Bishop of Zanzibar for seven years, and then Bishop of Northern Rhodesia for a term of five years. During his three African episcopates Hine confirmed 6,114 persons and estimated that he had traveled 12,500 miles on foot. Northern Rhodesia became a British protectorate in 1924, and it is now a part of the Province of Central Africa. Masasi, the fourth U.M.C.A. diocese was separated in 1926.

Eastern Equatorial Africa. Greatly moved by Livingstone's death in 1873, the explorer, Henry Morton Stanley, besought England to send missionaries to the Uganda country on the shores of Lake Victoria Nyanza. The Church Missionary Society accepted the challenge with the result that a small party, headed by the heroic Alexander Mackay, left England in 1876, but only he and one companion, C. T. Wilson, finally reached Uganda. One of the group had died and two were murdered, but in 1879 five more missionaries came out to join Mackay. They were all in great danger due to the hostility of the natives and also to the bitter opposition of the Moslems and the Roman Catholic missionaries, who did their best to turn the King, Mtesa, against the newcomers. Mtesa, bewildered by the strife and suspicions of white men anyway, decided to return to the religion of his fathers, but he allowed the missionaries to stay.

It was with the object of reinforcing this initial mission that James Hannington was consecrated in England as the first Bishop of Eastern Equatorial Africa on Saint John Baptist Day, 1884; and he was enthroned at Mombasa in February of the following year. He was not unfamiliar with Africa, since he had made a journey into the interior from Mombasa in 1883 before being invalided home. Following Krapf's strategy, Hannington's plan was to establish a series of mission stations from Mombasa west to Lake Victoria Nyanza by way of Mount Kilimanjaro. The Bishop accordingly set out on his long journey to Uganda, ignorant of the fact that Mtesa had died and that his eighteen-year-old son, Mwanga, had succeeded to the throne. Fearing the approach of another white man from the coast, and fearful for his kingdom, Mwanga ordered his soldiers to kill the Bishop when the latter reached the borders of his land in October of

110

1885. Hannington met his end with superb courage, saying to the warriors as they crowded around to plunge in their spears, "Go tell your king that I am dying for the people of Buganda, and that I have purchased the road to Uganda with my life."

This martyrdom was followed by a fierce persecution of the small band of native Christians who met torture and death with noblest fortitude, firm in their new-found faith. One of them, Robert Munyaga, who had his limbs cut off one by one and roasted before his eyes, remained steadfast to the end. For a time Mackay was the sole missionary left, and finally Mwanga forced him to go to the south side of the Lake where he continued his translation of the Scriptures into the Buganda tongue.

The second bishop, H. P. Parker, died in 1888, only eighteen months after his consecration and before he could reach Uganda; but his successor, Alfred R. Tucker, was blessed with an episcopate of eighteen years in Africa during which period immense changes took place. After spending some time at Mombasa and Zanzibar, Tucker started on his initial journey to Uganda in July, 1890; it was a distance of eight hundred miles from the coast, every mile of which had to be done on foot. The party of nine Europeans and 2,500 native porters carrying food and supplies averaged only ten or twelve miles a day over deserts, through forests and swamps. They survived these natural dangers and additional hazards of hostile tribes and fever and finally reached Mengo, the capital of Uganda, at the end of December, 1890.

In spite of incredible difficulties, the Uganda Mission gained many converts and by the end of 1892 a great church had been built outside the capital on Namirembe Hill (The Hill of Peace), which housed five thousand people. It was here on December 31, 1892, that Tucker buried the bones of Hannington, which he had discovered in a village grave not far from where the martyred bishop died. Christian work in Uganda was greatly helped when the British Parliament at last declared Uganda to be a protectorate and took the country over from the Imperial British East Africa Company. The little Christian flock of some two hundred in 1890 had grown in 1908 to 63,000, while in 1914 it was almost 100,000. This latter figure has more than tripled to date. These spectacular results were accomplished not alone by the English missionaries, for these were greatly helped by the increasing number of native teachers and clergy who helped evangelize the country to the east and west.

The work along the coast was also the responsibility of the Bishop of Eastern Equatorial Africa, for he spent a great deal of time, between journeys to Uganda, in founding and visiting missions in what are now the dioceses of Mombasa, Masasi, and Zanzibar. The goal of the Church in this area, to develop a native ministry, has been notably successful for the great majority of the clergy in Central Africa today are natives. This is all the more remarkable because the first native baptism as distinct from slave baptisms did not take place until 1865 in Zanzibar, and it was not until 1879 and 1890 respectively that the first native ordinations to the diaconate and priesthood were held.

The present seven dioceses in Eastern Equatorial Africa are currently under the jurisdiction of the Archbishop of Canterbury, although it is likely that a Province of East Africa will be constituted before too long. The dioceses all hold synods, but not all as yet have a formal constitution.

THE PROVINCE OF WEST AFRICA

*In the Name of God. Amen. Forasmuch as the Bish-
ops of the Diocese of Sierra Leone, the Diocese on the Niger,
the Diocese of Accra, the Diocese of Lagos, and the Diocese
of Gambia and the Rio Pongas, have by their signatures decreed and declared that their Dioceses are united in the Province of West Africa; We, Geoffrey, by Divine Providence
Lord Archbishop of Canterbury, do solemnly ratify and confirm the same, and do now relinquish all metropolitical
jurisdiction over the separate Dioceses of the Province, save
in so far as is determined in the Articles of the Constitution
of the said Province.*[15]

With these solemn words the Dioceses in West Africa became a new and fully autonomous Province of the Anglican
Communion on Sunday, April 15, 1951. It was a far cry from
that day two hundred years before, when one Thomas Thompson, an S.P.G. Missionary in North America, asked for and
obtained a transfer to the Coast of Guinea in 1751. He
stayed five years; and one result was that a chief's son,
Philip Quaque, was sent to England to be educated. The
young man was ordained in 1765 and returned to be a missionary to his people; he appears to have been the first of
any non-European race to be ordained in the Anglican
Church.

During the first seventy years of the nineteenth century
Christian churches from Europe and North America sent a
constant stream of missionaries to the west coast of Africa,
known as the Slave Coast. The toll of lives was heavy, and
not many white men lived more than a few years in the
hostile climate. More than one hundred missionaries died in

Sierra Leone within twenty-five years, and it is literally true that the Church has been built in that country on the graves of an uncounted company of men and women who volunteered for, and persisted in, the dangerous task of planting the Gospel in West Africa.

Before the coming of the missionaries, the slave trade was the dominant and unchallenged business on the West Coast. It was begun by European powers in the sixteenth century for the plantations of America and the West Indies, and it was a huge business: during the century preceding 1786 more than two million slaves were imported to the British Colonies. In a single year, 1771, almost two hundred slave ships left English ports destined for Africa and the Colonies, with quarters for more than 47,000 slaves.

The area which was to embrace the Province of West Africa is a large one, stretching from the British colony of Gambia at almost the westernmost point of the Continent to the southeast corner of Nigeria. This is as far as from New York to Cuba.

Although, as we have seen, S.P.G. was first in the field both on the Gold Coast and later at Sierra Leone, it was C.M.S. which was finally to concentrate its efforts in West Africa, and write a singularly successful chapter in Christian missions. Sierra Leone had belonged to Portugal since the middle of the fifteenth century, but it became an increasingly notorious center for slaving, which caused it to be taken over towards the end of the eighteenth century by the newly-formed English Sierra Leone Company, of which William Wilberforce was a director. Shortly afterwards, in 1808, the British Government made it a Crown Colony, ousted the slavers, forbade slaving in that territory, and began a settlement at Sierra Leone for liberated slaves. Enforcing the ban against the Trade was extremely difficult, however, for as late as 1838 more than one thousand slaves a day sailed from West Africa from hundreds of small ports. A system of coast patrol was in effect; and whenever an English cruiser overhauled a slaver, she took the human cargo to Sierra Leone. This solved only part of the problem, for the missionaries took care of many freed slaves. But since they came from many parts of the coast and spoke different languages, the task of the missionaries was not a simple one. The Sierra Leone Mission, begun in 1809, cared for hundreds of these unfortunate people; and as a result many were converted.

Sierra Leone became a diocese in 1852 and its first Bishop, E. O. Vidal, confirmed three thousand persons before he died after a three years episcopate. He also ordained two natives for work in Yorubaland, the area back of Lagos. Although the first three bishops had a combined episcopate of but eighteen years, the work flourished; and by 1861 there were nine parishes in Sierra Leone, each one with a native pastor. Before the end of the century the diocese had twenty-three native clergy and more than fourteen thousand members.

As it turned out, the area for the next great missionary advance was in the country around Lagos and up the Niger River. Moreover, the romantic story of the C.M.S. to the Niger River may be told largely in terms of one remarkable man, Samuel Adjai Crowther. The story begins on a spring day in 1822 when Captain Henry G. Leeke of H.M.S. *Myrmidon* captured a slaver off the Guinea Coast and took the released slaves to Sierra Leone. One of the slaves was a young boy from Oshogun in Yorubaland named Adjai, who had been separated from his mother and captured with others when the slavers burned their village. Young Adjai went to school at the Sierra Leone Mission where he was baptized, and later on he attended Fourah Bay College, which C.M.S. had opened in 1827 to develop native Christian leadership. Fourah Bay became an effective institution and produced many leaders in the Church over the years. From 1840 to 1860 the college was given notable leadership by an American priest, Edward Jones, and in 1876 it became affiliated with Durham University.

The mystery of the River Niger was solved about this time, for the river which began by running from west to east turned first southeast and then south before it emptied in a gigantic delta into the Gulf of Guinea. Until 1830 Europeans had supposed the "west to east river" connected with the Nile. Christian missionary strategists immediately saw the importance of this discovery, for they perceived that the Niger, like the Yang-tse in China, would provide a natural highway for the Gospel to the hinterland of Africa.

Young Crowther went up the river with the first exploring expedition in 1841, which showed that the Niger was navigable for a longer distance than the ships could then reach; one native missionary named Simon Jonas was left at the town of Ibo, and to him belongs the honor of beginning Christian missions on the River. Some years ensued before this beginning could be followed up; but in the meantime opportunity beckoned in another place. Crowther had gone to England after taking part in the first Niger expedition, and he was ordained there in 1843, returning to Africa that same year. In the meantime liberated slaves, some of them Christians, were making their way back from Sierra Leone to Abeokuta inland from Lagos. This determined C.M.S. first to begin a mission there before tackling the Niger, with the result that Crowther and a party of missionaries started work in Yorubaland, and a church was built in Abeokuta.

It was while Crowther was working here that he found his aged pagan mother from whom he had been separated for twenty-five years, and he had the joy of bringing her to baptism, for she was in his first class of converts in 1848. He also began translating parts of the New Testament into the Yoruba language at this time.

The work went forward, but tribal warfare together with the determined opposition of the slavers caused so much havoc that the British finally took Lagos in 1851, an event which dealt a fatal blow to the Trade in that area; Lagos was formally annexed in 1861. C.M.S. opened missions in Lagos and, beyond Abeokuta, at Ibadan where a devoted missionary couple, David Hinderer and his wife, stayed for seventeen years. Lagos became a C.M.S. headquarters from 1851 onwards, and a number of churches were built. Twenty years later there were several thousand Christians in that area.

Crowther joined a second Niger expedition in 1854, which this time got six hundred miles up the river. This convinced C.M.S. that their planned strategy was sound, so in 1857 a third "exploratory-missionary" expedition went up the river. This time Crowther took a small African staff with him, which he left to work at Onitsha, and this event marks the real beginning of the Niger Mission. A little later the boat was wrecked and the party had to wait a year before being rescued; but Crowther spent the time to good advantage going up and down the river talking with various chiefs, preaching, and getting mission sites. On the way back to the sea, the Onitsha Mission was found flourishing and the chief friendly. All of this pioneer work was carried on under tremendous handicaps which included inter-tribal warfare and slaving activities, to say nothing about the customs of human sacrifice, the worship of lizards, and the killing of twin babies—with all of which the missionaries had to deal.

The area obviously needed a chief shepherd, for the Bishop of Sierra Leone was two thousand miles away. Moreover, it needed someone who could stand the climate. Bishop Vidal had visited Lagos, Abeokuta, and Ibadan in 1854, and while there had confirmed six hundred converts and ordained three white missionaries and two Africans. He died on the way back before reaching Freetown. Bishop Bowen also made a visitation five years later; and he, too, confirmed several hundred persons and opened a church at Abeokuta. Much more could be done if the area had a bishop of its own, and it is to the great credit of Henry Venn, the C.M.S. secretary for the West African field, that he suggested and urged the authorities at home to appoint Crowther for the new bishopric. Accordingly, the former slave boy was called to England where he was consecrated the first Bishop of the Niger Territories at Canterbury Cathedral on St. Peter's Day, 1864. One of the congregation on that notable occasion was Admiral Sir Henry G. Leeke, who had commanded the *Myrmidon* on that spring day forty-two years before. Crowther was quite tireless and threw himself immediately into the building up of the Niger Missions. As the years went by, a paddle steamer called, appropriately, the *Henry Venn,* was provided for his transportation. He died at Lokoja on the last day of 1891 at a great age. He goes down in the history of Christian missions as a great pioneer who left a large African Church in Nigeria.

After Crowther's death, the two dioceses of Lagos and the Niger were united into Western Equatorial Africa with a white bishop and two African suffragans. It is interesting that in the century 1841 to 1940 the Church in West Africa

118

had fourteen native bishops. It was in the latter part of the nineteenth century that St. Andrew's College was opened at Oyo in Yoruba for the training of teachers, catechists, and clergy; it has proved to be a most important institution over the years. Some idea of the growth of the Church in the Diocese of Lagos may be seen by comparing the statistics of thirty years: in 1900 there were 2,449 baptized members, while in 1930 the number had grown to 109,345.

The Church's educational work in the Province has been and is very considerable; for if Anglican and other Christian institutions were to be taken away, "the greater part of education in British West Africa would vanish." [16] The work done with lepers has also been noteworthy: in Nigeria alone the greater part of leprosy relief and control has been pioneered by the Christian Churches. The Anglicans have a great leper settlement, with schools and a church, at Oji River in the center of Onitsha Province; it has sixty outstations with some 8,000 patients. While it was nationalized in 1945, the Church keeps control over the religious life of the settlement.

Because of its C.M.S. history Nigeria has been particularly interested in Christian reunion. As early as 1905 the Church of Scotland, the Anglicans, and the Niger Delta Protestants agreed to boundaries for their work; and in 1909 the Methodists joined them. A Christian Council of Nigeria was formed in 1930, and three years later they drew up a definite scheme of union based on the South India proposals; this Draft was completed in 1937. By 1946 Anglicans, Methodists, and Presbyterians had produced an Eastern Nigerian Plan of reunion which is now before those Churches in Western Nigeria. For the furtherance of this plan a Nigerian Church Union Committee was formed in 1947.

In 1944, ten West African bishops held a historic conference. This conference had been urged upon them by William Temple, and it was attended by the Archbishop of Capetown. After thoughtful discussion, they recommended the formation of a Province of West Africa. This came to pass, as we have seen, in 1951 when the Archbishop of Canterbury, Dr. Fisher, relinquished jurisdiction and inaugurated the new Province. He was the first Archbishop of Canterbury to set foot on West Africa. The new Province promptly elected its first Archbishop. Once again, an autonomous Anglican province came into being before any self-governing nation in that area, for the Gold Coast did not become Ghana until March 6, 1957.

There are now nine dioceses, each with its diocesan, while five of the nine have assistant bishops. The Church membership of the Province is growing steadily, no mean achievement considering the hazards of the early years and the short history of little more than a century. The dioceses in this Province have had outstanding success in missionary endeavor, and have used thousands of lay people in this work.

THE MISSIONARY DISTRICT OF LIBERIA

Liberia is the only area on the Continent of Africa where the American Church is working. It began soon after the American Colonization Society (founded in 1816) began to take slaves from the United States to Liberia. However, the Church undertook no permanent work there until 1835 when it began a mission at Monrovia, and this was followed by opening several other stations. By 1851 one of the staff, John Payne, a seminary classmate of China's Bishop Boone, was consecrated the first missionary Bishop of Liberia, and he served for twenty years, during which time the work grew and prospered. It was during Payne's episcopate, in the year 1862, that the United States finally acknowledged Liberia's independence, fifteen years after Liberia had announced it.

Following Payne there came two bishops who served for only short terms; one of them was John Gottlieb Auer, a Jew by birth whose promising work was cut short by an early death. The Church then made the choice of a Negro for the episcopate and consecrated Samuel David Ferguson in 1885. His thirty-one years in office saw the founding of Cuttington Collegiate Institute and Seminary at Cape Palmas, which meant that young men could henceforth be trained for the ministry in Liberia. When Ferguson died he had twenty-six Liberian clergy. Soon afterwards a native Vai, Theophilus Momolu Gardiner, became suffragan to the new Bishop Overs. Gardiner had been the first Vai to be ordered priest, and he was the first native to be consecrated a bishop in Liberia.

The Order of the Holy Cross came in 1922 and greatly strengthened the work by going to the interior at Bolahun. The Sisters of the Holy Name followed in 1931, and together the communities operate parishes as well as schools for boys and girls. Nearby is St. Joseph's Hospital, the only one in that entire large area.

St. Timothy's Hospital at Robertsport began in 1916 in a very small way, but it grew tremendously over the years chiefly as a result of the devoted work of Dr. Werner Junge. Today there is a school of nursing, a clinic, and a leper colony attached to the general hospital. The school of nursing and the hospital were sold to the Republic of Liberia in 1956.

An American Negro, Bravid Washington Harris, became the eighth Bishop of Liberia in 1945. His threefold pro-

121

gram of evangelism, education, and medical care have made a great impact on the country. Cuttington College, which had been closed since 1925, was moved to a new and healthier location at Suakoko where it trains clergy, agricultural students, and those who work on animal husbandry. There is still much to be done in welding together the great majority of the population who live away from the coast and the descendants of the returned slaves who live mostly in the coast cities.

The Missionary District of Liberia obviously belongs in the Province of West Africa, for it is contiguous to the adjacent dioceses that comprise the Province of West Africa; and it is a principle of Anglicanism that neighboring dioceses should be grouped in provinces as soon as possible.

THE CHURCH IN NORTH AFRICA

Egypt. This missionary diocese, founded in 1920, is one of the youngest in the Anglican Church, although C.M.S. had been working there since 1825. Nationalism, Moslems, and the bewildering variety of Christian bodies in the land all present formidable problems. However, the Anglican Church in Egypt has had a special work to do, for it has been a valuable agency in bringing together the Orthodox, Armenians, Copts, and Presbyterians in a Fellowship of Unity.

The Church also has chaplaincies in the large cities of Egypt and these form an important aspect of the total work. The third phase of Anglican effort centers at the Collegiate Church in Cairo which was consecrated in 1938; it ministers to both Europeans and native Egyptians. All English missionaries, including the Bishop, were expelled in 1956 following the Franco-British invasion; but it is hoped that this is but a temporary set-back to the work.

North Africa. This bishopric was separated from the large diocese of Sierra Leone in 1936; its formation as a diocese became possible due to the work and interest in that area of the Bible Churchmen's Missionary Society. The Bishop is appointed by the Archbishop of Canterbury, and the Society pays his stipend. Headquarters are at Tangier, and the jurisdiction embraces the Moroccos, Tunisia, Algeria, Tangier, Tripoli, and the Canary Islands. It is currently under the care of the Bishop of Gibraltar.

The Sudan. This Diocese, created in 1946, has its center at Khartoum, where the Anglicans have played an important role in bringing together the various non-Roman Churches in that area. The jurisdiction covers Aden, Abyssinia, and Eritrea, besides the Sudan.

THE MISSIONARY DIOCESE
OF MAURITIUS

The seven hundred and twenty square mile island of Mauritius, lying some five hundred miles east of Madagascar, was discovered by the Portuguese in the early sixteenth century; later it came under the French, but in 1810 the British captured it and the neighboring Seychelles. After the Napoleonic Wars, the British Government made a treaty with the French which included a pledge to support the Roman Catholic Church on the island.

We are told that a British missionary, on sick leave from India, held services in Port St. Louis in 1830, and that he also visited the Seychelles on his way back from furlough where he baptized almost five hundred persons, most of them slaves, in four days. More work was done over the next decade, but opposition from the Roman Catholics was so intense that Anglican missionary work had to be abandoned temporarily. However, by 1843 a permanent mission began in the Seychelles under a priest named de la Fontaine; and when Bishop Chapman of Colombo visited the islands in 1850, he found that twelve hundred had been baptized in the seven year period. Sixty were confirmed during the Bishop's visit and a little later two churches were built and consecrated.

The abolition of slavery in Mauritius in 1834 caused both S.P.G. and C.M.S. to begin work, and they established a number of schools for emancipated slaves. Hundreds of converts were made chiefly among the Indian coolie class.

Finally, when Mauritius was made a diocese in 1854, its first bishop, V. W. Ryan, gave able leadership, for within eight years seven church buildings were erected and the number of clergy had increased to fourteen. During the nineteenth century large numbers of Indians came over to work on the sugar plantations, so that by the end of that century they made up two-thirds of the population. Under these new circumstances, Indian Christians came over to help evangelize their compatriots; and in 1866 the first Tamil deacon, John Baptiste, was ordained. Some idea of the problems involved may be seen in the fact that at that particular service the Holy Communion was administered in four languages. The very mixed population now makes it necessary for the Church to minister to the people in seven languages: English, French, Tamil, Telegu, Hindu, Bengali, and Chinese. The population has declined slightly during the

124

present century, but there still remain more than a quarter of a million non-Christians on the Islands. The Cathedral of St. James was consecrated in 1850 and is still in use; certainly it must be unique among the cathedrals of the world in that it was once a powder magazine!

THE MISSIONARY DIOCESE
OF MADAGASCAR

For two hundred years the French tried to take this large island away from the Portuguese, who had discovered it in 1506; they finally succeeded in 1885, and it has remained a French possession to the present day.

The London Missionary Society (Congregational) opened up work in 1818, and they were the first non-Roman Christians to undertake work in Madagascar. There was every indication of success for this venture until Queen Ranavalona proscribed Christianity from 1835 until her death in 1861. Upon the accession of a new king, Radama II, the ban was lifted and the L.M.S. missionaries returned to their work as did also the Roman Catholics. The Congregationalists discovered to their joy that many of their flock had been faithful in spite of persecution; in fact, they found more than twenty thousand members when they returned.

The Bishops of Capetown and Mauritius attended the coronation of the new ruler, and shortly after this, in 1864, S.P.G. and C.M.S. sent missionaries to work on the north and east coasts. The Church of England soon wished to consecrate a bishop for Madagascar, but so much opposition developed from the Congregationalists that Archbishop Tait of Canterbury advised S.P.G. to go to the Scottish Episcopal Church, just as the American Churchmen had done a century before. Accordingly, R. K. Kestell-Cornish was consecrated the first Anglican Bishop of Madagascar in 1874 at Edinburgh by the Scottish bishops. He worked faithfully in his island diocese for twenty-two years, and in a short time several thousand Malagasy had become Anglicans. He also built the beautiful St. Laurence Cathedral in Tananarive in 1889. The first edition of a Malagasy Prayer Book in 1878 did much to teach the new converts common habits of worship, while a school for the training of native Christian leaders was begun in the same year. The Church grew considerably during the twentieth century, and it now has two bishops, one of them a national, for in 1956 Jean Marcel was consecrated at Lambeth Palace Chapel as Assistant Bishop of Madagascar. The new bishop is not only the first national to be made a bishop; he also belongs to a Church family for he has five brothers and a nephew in the priesthood. Today Madagascar has sixty priests, only four of whom are English S.P.G. missionaries.

India, Pakistan, Burma and Ceylon; the East Indies

India, Pakistan, Burma and Ceylon; the East Indies

THE CHURCH OF INDIA, PAKISTAN, BURMA AND CEYLON

The peninsular subcontinent of India is the same size as Europe, but its four hundred millions of people live mostly in small villages, and they speak some two hundred different languages. As early as the eighth century Moslem invaders from Afghanistan and Western Turkestan came down through the Khyber Pass to the northwest part of India, and over the years the invasions increased to such a degree that by 1206 the Moslems had captured Delhi. These Moslems ruled until the coming of the Moguls, who consolidated their power until the sixteenth century when Akbar the Great made himself supreme ruler (1556-1605) over a large part of India. It will be observed that for almost a thousand years the original Hindu population became increasingly subject to the powerful Moslem minority, a fact which explains much of India's subsequent history.

There is an enduring legend that the apostle St. Thomas first preached the Gospel in India, and that he laid down his life there in the year A.D. 52. Whether or not this legend is true, there is sufficient evidence to show that there were groups of Syrian Christians on the Malabar (West) coast by the fourth century of our era. The Moslem conquests noted above would account for the lack of missionary expansion of these Syrian Christians, for the next person to visit India with the Good News was St. Francis Xavier, who, in mid-sixteenth century, spent over four years preaching there with the aid of an interpreter. He succeeded in baptizing many thousands of converts, and was followed about 1600 by one Robert de Nobili, who taught a Brahminized form of Christianity. The Portuguese had gained control of the region around Goa towards the end of the fifteenth century, so that the missionary efforts of Xavier and de Nobili were backed by the arms and the authority of the King of Portugal. With the subsequent rise to power of the Dutch and the British, Roman Catholicism in India faded away with Portugal's decline.

On the last day of the year 1600 Queen Elizabeth I of England granted a charter to a private company of merchants for purposes of trade in India and the East Indies; this company, known as the "East India Company," began that year a connection with India that was to last for two and a half centuries. The Company founded a small trading post at Surat, north of Bombay, in 1614, despite the strong opposition of the Dutch and within a decade eleven other trading posts had been established. These "factories" as they were called, were concessions only; they were permitted to exist by the Great Mogul to whom the Company paid rent.

During these early days the existence of the factories was oftentimes precarious due to the hostility of the reigning Mogul. Nevertheless, the Company grew in power and finally it began to fortify its factory at Madras in 1640, and then the factories at Hugli near Calcutta in 1651. Thus the

English had full control of Madras by 1640, of Bombay in 1662, and of Calcutta in 1690.

The Company appointed regular chaplains to take care of its employees, and although the supply was never equal to the need, it was in this way that Anglican work began in India. St. Mary's Church in Madras was built in 1681 in great measure by local subscription, while St. Anne's Church was erected in Calcutta by 1709. Very little was done about evangelizing the Hindus because the duties of the chaplains were supposed to center about the Company's employees. However, the founding of S.P.C.K. and S.P.G. at this time brought about in England an increasing awareness of the Church's missionary responsibility with the result that increasing provision was made for work among the natives as the eighteenth century wore on.

King Charles II had received Bombay from Portugal in 1661 as a part of the Infanta Catherine's dowry, and he turned over this collection of swampy islands to the Company which—in spite of Dutch, Roman Catholic, and Mahratta opposition—developed the area into a strong and fortified town. By 1708 special provisions were made for educational and Christian work in that area, and a church was built in 1718 under the supervision of Chaplain Cobbe.

The last important Great Mogul had died in 1707, an event which threw India into anarchy, and also opened the way for a struggle to the death between England and France for the great prize. General Dupleix was inspired with the vision of establishing a great French Empire in India, founded on the ruins of the Mogul Empire, but he and his ally, Siraj-ud-daula, the ruler of Bengal, were decisively defeated by the brilliant generalship of Clive, who was the commander of the Company's private army. In the course of the war the settlement and church at Calcutta were destroyed, but with the successful conclusion of hostilities the town was re-occupied, the factory rebuilt, and a new church erected in 1770.

By this time the Company's red and white striped flag was a familiar sight along the world's sea lanes and in many harbors of North America, as well as in the Far East. From a small trading concern the Company had now grown into a great institution with its own armed merchant fleet and army.

Although Warren Hastings, the Company's Governor-General in India in 1773, laid down the rule that all missionary efforts were to be discouraged, there was a growing concern for the souls of the native peoples. Because of this official hostility, S.P.G. and S.P.C.K. were obliged to support the Danish mission at Tranquebar where the number of native Christians grew from 3,700 in 1740 to 18,000 by 1800. Even the great Baptist missionary, William Carey, was obliged to take refuge in the Danish mission at Serampore to escape the hostility of the Company towards missionary efforts. At the same time, the Company used a number of Lutherans for its own chaplains, one of the most distinguished of them being a German, Christian Schwartz (1726-1798). The noble Henry Martyn, who went to India as a Company chaplain, also belongs in the roster of the great Christians of the nineteenth century. He arrived in India in 1806; and although he spent little more than four years there, he preached and founded schools at Patna and Cawnpore, in addition to translating the New Testament into Urdu.

It was another chaplain, Claudius Buchanan, who was in

India from 1797 onwards, who both in his writings and by his speeches called attention to the need for episcopal supervision of the Church's work in India.

The Evangelical Revival in England and the founding of C.M.S. in 1799 awoke England from its spiritual sloth, and when the Company's charter came up for renewal in 1813, the great William Wilberforce was able to insist that the new charter should make the Company responsible for preaching and teaching the Christian faith. The directors of the Company were ordered to "direct and cause to be paid, certain established salaries to such Bishops and Archdeacons" as might be appointed to India.

A bill went through Parliament establishing the bishopric of Calcutta in 1814, the person chosen for this arduous honor being the Archdeacon, the vicar of St. Pancras in London, Thomas Fanshaw Middleton. Consecrated at Lambeth Palace Chapel at a very private service in May, the forty-five-year-old bishop arrived in Calcutta the following November, to find himself at the head of thirty-two clergy for the whole of India and a jurisdiction which included Ceylon, the East Indies, Australia, and Tasmania!

Middleton's task was further complicated by the fact that his clergy were of two kinds: Company chaplains who were appointed to their stations and paid by the Company; and missionaries, mostly Lutherans, who were appointed by various missionary societies in England and were largely subject to their jurisdiction. It was a situation calculated to daunt a lesser man than the Bishop. Nevertheless, he undertook immediately a visitation of the southern and western areas of his vast jurisdiction. The visitation took a whole year and even then he had covered only two-thirds of his responsibility in

India. Among Middleton's great achievements is the foundation of Bishop's College in Calcutta, in 1820, for the education of Indian clergy.

Reginald Heber was already famous as a hymn-writer when he succeeded Middleton to the See of Calcutta in 1823. From his arrival until his untimely death in 1826, the Bishop was traveling, preaching, teaching, and confirming. In Madras he confirmed five hundred and seventy-eight people in one day, an indication both of the need and the opportunity. Heber's first visitation lasted sixteen months, and his death occurred during his second one.

The tremendous size of the jurisdiction, together with the unhealthy climate, took its grim toll: two more bishops, James and Turner, were worn out before relief came. However, when the Company's charter came up for renewal in 1833, provision was made for the creation of two more dioceses. The great Daniel Wilson had gone to the See of Calcutta in 1832, and three years later a bishop was consecrated for Madras and one for Bombay in 1837. Colombo was the next diocese to be created and that in 1845. These events made Wilson the Metropolitan and the Church in India a quasi-province, although it was a century away from self-government.

Wilson, who was a contemporary of Heber at Oxford, was outspokenly courageous in condemning the recognition of caste within the Church, and he was obliged to challenge the assumed authority of C.M.S., which body attempted to continue appointing clergy to posts without consulting the Bishop. Wilson built a cathedral in Calcutta, and was so vigorous that at the age of seventy-three he made the four-thousand-mile journey to Sarawak to consecrate a church there.

The Indian Mutiny of 1857, confined mainly to Bengal, Central India, and the Northwest, ended the rule of the East India Company and caused India to be taken over by the Crown by the Proclamation of 1858. Calcutta, which remained the capital until 1911, was fortunate to have two great bishops between 1858 and 1876 in the persons of George Edward Cotton and Robert Milman. Cotton, the author of the missionary prayer which begins, "O God, who has made of one blood all nations of men" (Book of Common Prayer, p. 38), did notable work with schools for Anglo-Indian children. His death by accidental drowning on a visit to Assam was a great calamity. Milman, his successor, was a nephew of the great Dean of St. Paul's Cathedral, London. During his time the Punjab, the Central Provinces, Oudh, and Burma were added to the diocese of Calcutta, an extension of work which caused Milman to appeal to the American Church for aid in prophetic words: "The future of the world also is so much to all appearances in the hands of America that I feel myself bound to make no longer delay." [17] It was an eloquent appeal, but Milman received no material response.

The growth of the Church was quite remarkable from the end of the Mutiny to the end of the nineteenth century. In Madras alone the years from 1861 to 1898 saw an increase from some 40,000 to 122,000 baptized Anglicans. Likewise, the number of native Christians in British India increased sixty-six per cent between 1875 and 1895, an increase all the more remarkable when it is remembered that a native who adopted Christianity forfeited any inheritance and was ostracized from his family.

New dioceses were added, Lahore being formed in 1899 as a memorial to Bishop Milman, and Rangoon in the same year. In the latter place the Anglicans inherited much from

135

the work of Adoniram Judson, the famous Baptist missionary to Burma. Lucknow diocese was added in 1893; it was the region where the Westcott brothers came to form the beginnings of a Christian brotherhood.

In the central part of the country the diocese of Chota-Nagpur was set up in 1890; it was an area where Bishop Milman had received several thousand Lutheran aborigines in 1869, and they made up the core of the newly-formed diocese. A theological college founded here in 1879 has produced an effective native ministry. The diocese of Nagpur, set apart in 1902, is the especial care of the Episcopal Church of Scotland.

In the South, three dioceses were taken out of Madras: Travancore and Cochin in 1879, where a small group of Syrian Christians formed the nucleus of the Anglican group; Tinnevelly in 1896; and Dornakal in 1912. It was in the latter diocese that Bishop Azariah, the first national to be consecrated for the Indian Church, labored with great success. A Tamil, Azariah guided mass movements of natives into the Church, using clergy and hundreds of native catechists for this purpose. Azariah was able to inspire his workers with his own consecrated spirit, for it is estimated that between 1922 and 1934 some 28,000 caste converts alone were received into the Church. By 1930 there were over 200,000 Anglicans in the diocese of Dornakal.

A few decades after India became a British possession, currents of nationalism began to flow with gradually increasing vigor. As a result, from 1861 onwards the Imperial Government gave an increasingly large share of government to the Indians, until 1947 when India became an independent Dominion within the British Commonwealth, and 1950 when it became a republic.

Ten years before this, the Church of India, Burma, and

Ceylon had become a free and autonomous branch of the Anglican Church. Diocesan conferences had been held at intervals since Bishop Cotton had called the first one in 1863; but they had no authority, not even when they were called "synods," as they were from 1920 onwards. The Constitution of the Church, largely the work of Bishop Foss Westcott and his committee, makes provision for a General Council of bishops, clergy, and laity, but decisions on Faith and Order are left to the House of Bishops. The Archbishop of Calcutta remains the Metropolitan. Election to the episcopate is by the local Diocesan Council if it can elect by a clear majority; otherwise the Metropolitan and two other bishops make the selection from not more than four clergy whose names are presented to them from the Diocesan Council where the vacancy occurs.

Two recent events in India have had grave effects on the total life of the Church there. Pakistan became independent in 1948, and a Moslem State came into being where freedom of religion is guaranteed. However, the entire Christian population in Pakistan is less than nine per cent of the total population in the largest Moslem state in the world. Parts of the Lahore, Calcutta, and Barrackpore dioceses fall within the borders of Pakistan.

A second event of far-reaching importance occurred in 1947, when the four southern dioceses of the Church—Madras, Dornakal, Tinnevelly, and Travancore, with their half-million Anglicans—withdrew to join the Church of South India. This latter Church was formed by the merger of three groups: The South India United Church which itself was the result of an earlier merger of Presbyterian, Reformed, and Congregational Churches; the Methodist Church of South India; and the four Anglican dioceses. This Church of

South India is not at present in communion with the See of Canterbury, although the Lambeth Conference of 1948 gave it a qualified blessing. More recently, in 1955, the Joint Convocation of Canterbury and York acknowledged the bishops, priests, and deacons of the Church of South India to be true bishops, priests, and deacons of the Church of Christ. They also agreed that, under certain circumstances, laity of the Church of South India might receive communion in English Churches; and that by permission of the incumbent and the bishop, episcopally ordained priests of the Church of South India might celebrate the Holy Communion in an English parish church. The Episcopal Church of Scotland has taken similar action but with more careful safeguards around the reception of the Holy Communion. Further plans for Church union involving Anglicans in North India, Pakistan, and Ceylon are now being studied and will be presented to the Lambeth Conference of 1958.

The remaining Church of India, Pakistan, Burma and Ceylon has been gravely weakened by the withdrawal of the four southern dioceses where five-eighths of its former numerical strength resided. However, it has not been lacking in missionary outreach, particularly in the Nicobar Islands where Bishop John Richardson has labored with great effect.

A most significant event, and a milestone in the life of the Church, took place in 1950, when Bishop A. N. Mukerjee of Delhi was elected Archbishop of Calcutta and Metropolitan. For the first time a national of India, who had been educated, ordained, and consecrated in his own land, became the head of a Province.

Religious Communities have done much for the Church since the arrival of the Cowley Fathers in Bombay in 1874.

They were followed by the Wantage Sisters, the Cambridge Mission Brotherhood, the Oxford Mission to Calcutta, and others. Bishop's College became a theological school in 1918, and since that time has trained some two hundred nationals for Holy Orders. The Anglican Church still places great emphasis on education—out of forty Christian colleges in India and Pakistan, Anglicans are responsible for ten; and they share the responsibility with other Christian groups for six other Christian institutions.

The Church, which until recently used the 1662 Prayer Book, now has a Proposed Prayer Book containing an alternative Liturgy which is the equal of any in the Anglican Communion. A marked feature of this branch of the Anglican Church has been its great gift for worship; a gift which is reflected in the beauty of its Liturgy and in the devoutness of its members.

THE MISSIONARY DIOCESE OF BORNEO

One James Brooke, an Englishman, landed at Kuching in 1838. Three years later he had become Rajah of Sarawak, an area of 41,000 square miles on the northern coast of Borneo. Sarawak was made an independent state under the protection of Great Britain, and the Rajah immediately asked S.P.G. and C.M.S. to send missionaries. Since the population then consisted mostly of Sea Dyaks who were pirates, and Land Dyaks who were head hunters, together with numbers of both Malays and Chinese, there was an evident need for missionaries.

As it turned out, neither S.P.G. nor C.M.S. could undertake the work at the time, but a private society was organized, two men went out with their families, and they arrived at Kuching (the Malay word for "cat") in 1838. W. B. Wright and F. T. McDougall were the two missionaries, and one of them, McDougall, was both a priest and a doctor. The work prospered and so S.P.G. began to contribute both men and money by 1853. The aged Bishop Wilson made the long journey from Calcutta to consecrate St. Thomas Church, Kuching, in 1851, and four years later McDougall went to Calcutta to be consecrated first Bishop of Labuan. He was the first English colonial bishop to be consecrated outside of England. McDougall was a remarkable man and laid permanent foundations for evangelizing the nationals during his fourteen-year episcopate. Since he was a doctor as well as a clergyman, he was used to acting in a dual capacity, and upon one occasion, after conducting divine service, he amputated a man's leg.

Slowly, but surely, the influence of the Church prevailed, and a blackened human head was no longer regarded as a prized possession of a Land Dyak family. One Dyak named Remba, having been converted and baptized, returned to his own people and without the aid of missionaries taught the Faith to his people for ten years and built a church. Another convert, a Sea Dyak, the son of an old pirate chief, converted his whole tribe before asking a missionary to baptize almost two hundred well-instructed natives. Work also began with the Chinese in 1865 and, in spite of severe opposition from their families, hundreds were baptized. Bishop McDougall resigned in 1868 and was succeeded by W. Chambers, who had been working in Borneo since 1851. During his episcopate the Straits Settlements was added to Labuan and Sarawak, as the diocese was then named. Singapore became a separate diocese by 1909. Currently the work is flourishing, particularly in the Land Dyak area around

140

Kuching; and in 1956 the great new Cathedral of St. Thomas, Kuching, was dedicated, replacing the smaller century-old building. The large Chinese population in Kuching, many of whom are Anglicans, have been described as the backbone of the Church's work there.

THE MISSIONARY DIOCESE
OF SINGAPORE

The island of Singapore became a British possession in 1819 through a treaty made with the local sultan by the fabulous Stamford Raffles. It was in this way that the threatened control of the Eastern Archipelago by the Dutch was forestalled by the English. A representative of the East India Company, Raffles was chiefly interested in opening up trade, but he was by no means indifferent to Christian missions. He welcomed Bishop Middleton of Calcutta when the latter dignitary visited Penang in 1819, and he also contributed to the work of S.P.C.K.

From 1814 to 1869 Singapore and Borneo were part of the Diocese of Calcutta, but in the latter year Singapore, the Straits Settlements, and Borneo were formed into a separate diocese. Changes have been made in this arrangement from time to time, until today the Diocese of Singapore comprises Thailand, Java, Johore, Kelantan with Trengganu, Malacca, Negri Sembilan, North Perak, Pahang, Penang, Province Wellesley, Kedah and Perlis, Selangor, Singapore, South Perak, Cambodia, Laos, and Vietnam.

There are forty-four churches in the diocese, including the beautiful St. Andrew's Cathedral in Singapore where the services are conducted in English, Mandarin, and Malay. The population of this area is as diverse as it is anywhere in the world, which means that in addition to the above languages used in public worship, various congregations use Tamil, several Chinese dialects, Indian languages, Malayalam, and Hindustani. There are twenty-one clinics and two hospitals, the latter in the city of Singapore; there are also twenty-three church schools with a total of more than ten thousand pupils. Men are trained for the ministry at Trinity College, Singapore, an institution operated jointly by Anglicans, Methodists, and Presbyterians. The Anglicans live at nearby St. Peter's Hall, which gives them the additional and particular work necessary for ordination to the Anglican priesthood.

In 1955 an important conference of Anglican representatives from South East Asia was held in Hong Kong. The Advisory Council for Missionary Strategy asked them to meet and as a result of their deliberations there was created a regional organization known as the "Council of the Episcopal Church in South East Asia." This might well grow in the course of time into another province of the Church.

CHAPTER FIVE

Australasia

Australasia

THE CHURCH OF ENGLAND
IN AUSTRALIA AND TASMANIA

When the American Colonies were lost to England, the British Government selected far away Australia as the territory to which to transport English criminals. Captain Cook, when on his way home from New Zealand, landed at the southeast coast at Botany Bay in 1770 and claimed the land for his native country, calling it New South Wales. Eighteen years later a penal settlement landed at Botany Bay near the present city of Sydney; it consisted of eight hundred convicts with two hundred soldiers to look after them. The British Government had no thought for the spiritual welfare of the transportees, and it was only at the last moment before the same ship sailed for the Antipodes that William Wilberforce, Charles Simeon, and others prevailed upon the authorities to appoint a chaplain, without pay, for the unwelcome task. One Bible was also provided.

The penal colony landed at the end of January, 1788, and the completion of the then hazardous voyage was celebrated by the firing of guns and the issue of an extra ration of rum. The chaplain, one Richard Johnson, managed to build a church largely with his own hands—at a cost of some sixty-seven pounds over the next six years—but the convicts, now numbering some thirty-five hundred, promptly burned it down. The authorities immediately caused the convicts to build a new church, this time of stone, more perhaps with the object of keeping their charges occupied than from any interest in religion. In 1794 a very notable chaplain and missionary, Samuel Marsden, joined Johnson at Sydney and the following year the S.P.G. began work in Australia. From that time until 1900, the Venerable Society was to give over two hundred and fifty thousand pounds for work on the continent. Likewise, in the period 1820 to 1898, S.P.C.K. gave more than eighty-six thousand pounds, and C.M.S. gave great help to Marsden in his work throughout the colony. Marsden served faithfully and brilliantly in Australia and New Zealand until his death in 1838.

By 1817 five chaplains were ministering to a population now increased to 17,000, of whom 7,000 were convicts; sixteen years later the free population had grown to more than 17,000, while the convict population numbered 21,000. The transportation system was abolished for New South Wales in 1839, but it was operative in Tasmania until 1853, and it lingered on in Western Australia until 1868. The convict population caused continuing problems for years to come.

It was becoming obvious, even to the British Government, that the infant Church needed direction and organization; and in 1814 a small but unrealistic beginning was made when Australia was included in the newly constituted diocese of Calcutta. Ten years later Australia became an archdeaconry within the Diocese of Calcutta and it was given a resident archdeacon, one Thomas Hobbes Scott. However, it was the second archdeacon of New South Wales, William Grant Broughton, who was destined to play an immense part in the growth of the Australian Church. He left his post of chaplain at the Tower of London in 1829 and journeyed

146

to Australia where he had but twenty clergy, the fruits of fifty years of British colonization. He spent five active and arduous years traveling vast distances before being recalled to England for consecration in 1836 as the first and only bishop of the whole continent. The diocese was now subject to Canterbury instead of Calcutta.

Marsden gave great and loyal support to his bishop, in spite of the fact that he might well have expected to be in Broughton's place. They worked harmoniously together building churches and schools, activities which the government aided, since from 1790 onwards 400 acres were set apart in each township for religious and educational purposes. Because of this establishment, Broughton was a member of the Legislative Council, and that meant that both his legal and personal authority were considerable. Nor did the Bishop neglect other parts of his large jurisdiction, for Broughton visited Tasmania twice before the island was set aside as a separate diocese in 1842; evidently it needed special attention because in that year the convicts numbered 18,000 out of a total population of 60,000. The erection of three new dioceses of Melbourne, Adelaide, and Newcastle in 1847 did much to expedite the growth of the Church as well as to relieve Broughton. When the latter died early in 1853, during a visit to England, the Chief Justice of New South Wales said of him, "No man ever went down to his grave full of years and honor carrying with him more deservedly the respect and devotion of his fellow colonists. I believe that by all classes and by all sects no man in the Colony was more unreservedly respected than Bishop Broughton." [18] He is buried at Canterbury Cathedral.

Church work was begun at Melbourne in 1836, and at Adelaide about the same time; progress was rapid at the

147

latter place for early colonists gave two acres of land to the Church, an area which now is in the center of the city. To the north a former penal settlement at Moreton Bay, near what is now Brisbane, was opened to free settlement in 1843, and Broughton sent a chaplain there. Brisbane became a part of the newly-constituted diocese of Newcastle in 1847, and the first bishop, William Tyrrell, devoted the remaining thirty-two years of his life to the work there. Except for a journey to New Zealand and the Melanesian Mission, Tyrrell never left Australia. He often travelled 1500 miles by horse in the early days, and during his episcopate he built fifty-five churches, twenty parsonages, and a great many schools. S.P.G. backed the work vigorously, and so rapid was the growth that the Venerable Society withdrew all support in that area by 1880; Brisbane had become a separate diocese in 1859.

Expansion of the Church in Western Australia was much slower because of its isolation and great distance from the initial settlements. It is interesting that the first work done there was by Archdeacon Thomas Hobbes Scott, who, having been shipwrecked at Freemantle on his way home to England, capitalized on his misfortune, built a church there in 1829, and appealed to England for help. Bishop Short of Adelaide had Western Australia added to his jurisdiction in 1847, and while he visited the colony the next year, it was another decade before Perth had its own bishop. In 1872 the diocese held its first synod, just after the state gained representative government. Today the four western dioceses cover one-third of the continent where less than half a million people inhabit one million square miles.

The tremendous population growth which took place in the latter half of the nineteenth century was due largely to the discovery of gold, beginning at Ballarat in 1851. From a

148

population of 200,000 in 1845, Australia jumped to four million fifty years later. The attendant lawlessness and the continual shifts of population, caused by successive discoveries of gold in the north and west, were serious social phenomena which taxed the Church's resources to the utmost. Churches and schools were left partly built, prices rose, and half the population went wild with dreams of sudden wealth.

During the period from 1829 to 1892, the organized Church grew from one diocese to fourteen, from twenty clergy to eleven hundred, and from a Church membership numbered in the hundreds, to one and a half million. Even so, the clergy often had to minister to vast areas, as was the case in Ballarat, where there were but thirty-three clergy in 1875 to minister to a population of 250,000 scattered over an area half the size of England.

Since 1895 no less than eleven new dioceses have been added to the Church, making a total of twenty-five. These are divided into four provinces which are coterminous with the political states: New South Wales, Queensland, Victoria, and West Australia; each province has its own archbishop. Three dioceses, Adelaide, Tasmania, and Willochra, are not attached to any province at present.

A remarkable feature of the Australian Church has been its missionary outreach and concern. This impetus has come from the great missionary societies themselves, and also from the clergy and people of the Church. Both Broughton of Sydney and Selwyn of New Zealand were great Christian statesmen; and it was they who called an epochal conference at Sydney in 1850 that they might discuss with their brother bishops of Adelaide, Melbourne, Tasmania, and Newcastle two pressing questions. The first question related to the missionary responsibility of the Churches of Australia and New Zealand to other areas in the Pacific. The two leaders felt very strongly that the Church, not individual missionary societies, should take the responsibility for planning and prosecuting the total missionary endeavor. This is the same theory under which both the American and Canadian Churches operate.

The meeting at Sydney over a century ago resulted in the formation of the Australasian Board of Missions for work with the aborigines of Australia, the natives of islands near the continent, and the peoples of New Guinea, Melanesia, China, and Japan. If their reach exceeded their grasp, it was to the credit of the leaders of those infant Churches in the Antipodes still very much missions themselves.

As the Australian Church tended to direct its missionary program more and more, it came to terms with the independent societies, with the result that C.M.S., for instance, is represented in the Anglican Missionary Council of the General Synod.

Mission work began in New Guinea in 1886, and the Island became a missionary diocese attached to Australia seven years later. The work has gone steadily forward except for the disruption caused by World War II. New Guinea was the scene of many heroic rescues of Americans by Christian Papuans during the war, and it was at Gona Mission down the coast that ten Anglican Christians, white and black, were killed by the Japanese when the latter invaded the town in 1942. Some measure of the moral and spiritual progress within a few decades is indicated by the facts that it is still possible to talk with some of the older Christian men who were once cannibals, and that the Cathedral at Dogura was built recently by the Papuans on land that had been a fighting-ground for cannibals half a century before. The boundaries of the diocese have recently been extended to include eastern New Guinea, New Britain, New Ireland, Bougainville, and the Bismarcks.

The Conference of the six bishops in 1850 likewise gave attention to the problem of self-government for the Church in Australia and New Zealand.

The great distance from England, the example of self-government furnished by the Episcopal Church in the United States, and the far-sighted statesmanship of both Broughton and Selwyn made it inevitable that both the Australian and the New Zealand Churches should seek to order their own affairs. Selwyn succeeded rapidly in getting self-government for the Church in New Zealand in 1847, but the Australian Church has been less fortunate for it is still without a Constitution and complete self-government. The latter Church did set up a General Conference or Synod which was held at Sydney in 1872, and it arranged for subsequent General Synods to meet every five years. The president of the General Synod is always the Primate and is himself elected to that office from among the four metropolitans of the provinces. However, due to the fact that the Church has no Constitution, the General Synod cannot legislate for the dioceses, and therefore neither the General Synod nor the Primate has any real authority. The initial difficulty was that the Church was organized as a part of the Church of England; in fact it had the curious original title: "The United Church of England and Ireland in Australia and Tasmania"! However, this legal attachment to the Church of England was no real bar to self-government because the Australian Church simply needed to organize itself on the basis of a common agreement; this it has been unwilling to do to date. Several draft constitutions have been presented, debated, and rejected since 1926, and it was not until the Archbishop of Canterbury revised the proposed Constitution during his visit in 1950 that the document seems to have met with general approval. It was approved by the General Synod in 1955, and now has to be submitted to the dioceses and to the five Parliaments for their approval or rejection. Apparently the reason for this long delay in reaching autonomy is due to an unreasoning fear on the part of substantial minorities in each diocese that autonomy might change the character of the Church. This might be true, but change is not necessarily a bad thing.

A notable feature of Australian Church missionary work is the Bush Brotherhoods which were designed to minister effectively to the people who live in the "outback," that is, the vast sparsely-settled areas of that country. Clergy and laymen who join these Bush Brotherhoods must be willing to serve the Church in that work for at least five years, and the Bush Brothers live in community houses to which they return at intervals after spending their time ministering over their large "parishes." In some ways the Bush Brothers are reminiscent of the Methodist circuit riders of the American frontier days; it is a pity that the American Church did not use similar methods. The Brotherhood Community House often has an adjoining hospital and school.

In spite of a too great reliance on the Church of England for its top leadership and an unwillingness to cut itself loose from the Church of England as by law established, the Church of Australia has come a long way in little more than a century and a half, from a handful of convicts with a single chaplain to a Church which comprises twenty-five dioceses and 44 per cent of the total population.

THE PROVINCE OF NEW ZEALAND

High in the hills above Cape Farewell at the north-west corner of North Island, Captain Cook and his crew of H.M.S. *Endeavour* noticed a "lone wooden cross." The native Maoris said that it had been there a long, long time and sometimes they put flowers by it according to an ancient custom. Since the Dutch navigator Tasman had discovered New Zealand in 1642 and Cook landed there in 1769, per-haps unknown Christians had been there in the interim to preach to the fierce Maoris. We do not know.[19]

It was not until the nineteenth century that any effort was made to carry the Gospel to New Zealand, and it was the Reverend Samuel Marsden, a missionary in Australia, who first began work with the Maoris. He is the first re-corded man to hold a Christian service in New Zealand—by the sea at what is now Auckland, on Christmas Day, 1816. Marsden succeeded in interesting the C.M.S. in this new work, and they sent out the remarkable Henry Williams, a former Royal Navy man, who worked with the Maoris from 1822 until his death forty-five years later. Marsden and Williams together laid the foundations of the Church's work in New Zealand;[20] but it was an uphill affair, for the first eleven years saw no conversions. However, the years from 1833 to 1850 showed striking advance, with the former fierce warriors beginning to settle down to farming life. Bishop Broughton came from Australia to hold the first Maori confirmation in 1838, and by this time C.M.S. had thirty-five missionaries at work and fifty-one schools had been estab-lished.

With an amazing indifference to geography the British Government had included New Zealand in Broughton's

153

original jurisdiction of Australia and Tasmania. It was an impossibly large area as Broughton realized, and largely because of his representations, a separate bishop was appointed for New Zealand in 1841, the year after the country became a Crown Colony. The overseas Church was now in a period of rapid expansion, for additional bishops were needed in thirteen British possessions. However, since New Zealand stood first on the list, the thirty-two-year-old George Augustus Selwyn, curate of Windsor, was consecrated the first Bishop of New Zealand at Lambeth Palace Chapel in October, 1841. This young man, now the pastor of some thirty thousand Maoris and a few white settlers, knelt on the shore of Auckland, May 30, 1842, and on the following Sunday preached in the Maori tongue to the surprised delight of his congregation. He had learned the language on the long voyage out!

For the next twenty-five years Selwyn gave his brilliant and sagacious devotion to the organization and upbuilding of the Church in New Zealand and in the islands of the Pacific Ocean. When he left to become Bishop of Lichfield, England, in 1868, the Church in New Zealand was self-governing and largely self-supporting. This was due in largest measure to Selwyn's leadership.

The New Zealand Land Company was formed in England in 1839 for the purpose of encouraging emigration, but it took care not to repeat the mistake of allowing convicts to go out to the new land, as had been the case in Australia. However, the Company soon found itself at odds with the natives, for by the Treaty of Waitangi (1840) the Maoris agreed to accept the sovereignty of the British Crown on condition that they be treated on an equality with the whites. This treaty was annulled six years later by the Imperial

154

Parliament at the instigation of the Land Company and over the vigorous protests of Bishop Selwyn. Maori land was in effect expropriated, and the New Zealand story at this point is similar to the story of the United States Government and the American Indians. The white settlers wanted to develop their newly acquired land whereas the Maoris were nomadic people and were used to cultivating an area for a while and then moving on. Selwyn's last years in New Zealand were clouded by the outbreak of the Maori wars, which came about largely because of the intransigent attitude of the New Zealand Company towards the natives.

Because of difficulties with the Land Company, Selwyn settled at Waitami, some one hundred fifty miles north of Auckland, and there C.M.S. had its headquarters. Later he returned to Auckland where an industrial school for both white and Maori boys was started; by 1846 it had some one hundred thirty pupils. Selwyn knew the importance of developing a native ministry, so on his missionary journeys he always kept a sharp lookout for promising young native boys who could be given a Christian education and then sent back to convert their own people. Certainly the Bishop traveled extensively, for on one missionary journey alone he covered 2,277 miles, with some one hundred sixty-two of these accomplished on foot! He once remarked that he averaged about one candidate for confirmation for every mile of traveling! [21] The Bishop worked for the common good of both whites and natives, and he had the joy of ordaining his first Maori deacon after ten years of work in New Zealand.

Bishop Selwyn's notable missionary record is equalled by his ecclesiastical statesmanship, for soon after moving to Auckland, in 1844, he called together the first synod of clergy to meet in any Anglican Church since Convocation had been suspended in England in 1717. This synod was followed by another one three years later at which the Bishop outlined a proposed Constitution for the Church in New Zealand so that it could govern itself. The proposed Constitution was similar to that of the American Episcopal Church, and it stated clearly that the governing of the Church was to be accomplished by bishops, clergy, and laymen. As Selwyn said, "The terms of our cooperation . . . are simply these: that neither will I act without you, nor can you act without me." [22] The Constitution was promulgated in 1857 and the first General Synod of the Church took place in 1859 at Wellington. The Constitution, substantially unchanged, is in effect in the Church today, a monument to Selwyn's genius.

Selwyn had gone to England in 1854 to obtain legal sanction for the proposed changes in the Church's government, but his failure to obtain official permission only determined him the more to proceed, for he understood quite thoroughly that the Church in far-away New Zealand must be autonomous in order to grow. Selwyn was successful in obtaining three new dioceses: Christ Church in 1856, Wellington and Nelson in 1858, so that there were four bishops at the first General Synod of 1859. From that time onwards, bishops were both chosen by the New Zealand Church and also were consecrated in that country. The first of these was William Williams, first Bishop of Waiapu, who received consecration at the hands of his four brethren in 1859. Within a few years, the Church in New Zealand was to all intents and purposes separated from the supervision of the Church of England and had taken its place as an autonomous Church. By 1869 when the new See of Dunedin was erected, the Church had ten dioceses including the vast area of Melanesia.

John Coleridge Patteson, who had been working in the Melanesian Islands since 1854, followed Selwyn's lead by bringing native boys back to Auckland and then to Norfolk Island for Christian training; it was to Norfolk Island that the Government had recently transferred the descendants of the *Bounty* mutineers. These people provided one of the "most remarkable Confirmations in the history of the Church," for Selwyn records that at his visitation after they had arrived at Norfolk Island "the whole adult population of former Pitcairn Islanders, except those who were too feeble to attend, presented themselves to me in nine classes to be examined and confirmed." [23]

Patteson had heard the call to missionary work as a young boy at Eton College Chapel as he listened to Selwyn, the then newly appointed Bishop of New Zealand tell of the work he was to take up. Thirteen years later Patteson followed Selwyn to New Zealand, and after 1859 the whole burden of the Melanesian mission fell on Patteson's capable shoulders; two years later he was consecrated the first Bishop of Melanesia at the age of thirty-four. The work was bright with promise and no one could guess how swiftly tragedy would come. It is thought that one of the "blackbirders," or slavers, who regularly raided the island had impersonated the Bishop in a recent descent on the Island of Nukapu; at any rate, Bishop Patteson went ashore on Nukapu one day in 1871 alone and, of course, unarmed. He was welcomed and feasted by the natives, but while he was asleep afterwards, a native whose brother had been kidnapped by a "blackbirder" entered the hut and murdered the Bishop. Soon after, a native canoe was seen floating out with Patteson's body on it, with a palm branch of five knots placed upon his breast. Patteson's pectoral cross is worked into the altar of Selwyn College in Cambridge University to remind other generations of his martyrdom, and of the cause for which he died.

It was Bishop Selwyn's son, John Richardson Selwyn, who interpreted Patteson's death as a call to himself, for he went to Melanesia and speedily picked up the threads of his predecessor's work among the natives. Sailing alone and unarmed in the small boat *Southern Cross,* he went from island to island, visiting also the ill-fated Nukapu where he re-established contact with the natives. After four such years of missionary travel John Richardson Selwyn became second Bishop of Melanesia in 1877.

Another huge area which is the responsibility of the Church in New Zealand is the diocese of Polynesia, an area of seven and a half million square miles containing at least six hundred islands. Anglican work began at Levuka, the old capital of Fiji, in 1870, and the S.P.G. began to help in this area twelve years later. The first bishop was appointed in 1908 and there is a cathedral at Suva, the capital of Fiji. This is the Anglican Cathedral where each new day begins; for since it is close to the "date line" those who kneel before its altar at the early Eucharist lead the rest of Christendom in the worship of God as "the dawn leads on another day."

A great deal of work is still done with Maoris in New Zealand, most of whom are on the North Island, and there is a Maori bishop of Aotearoa. There is no color bar in New Zealand, and intermarriage between whites and natives is not looked upon as anything untoward. Many Maoris are ordained and either go back to work with their people or else work in mixed congregations.

The General Synod, which meets every three years, consists of three orders: bishops, priests, and laymen, and although they sit in one chamber, the consent of all three orders is necessary for all the acts of the Synod; the Diocesan Synods meet every year. The method used for electing a bishop is interesting. He is nominated by the Synod of the diocese, which Synod is presided over for the purpose by an outside bishop. The name decided upon is then submitted to the Archbishop, who in turn submits it to the diocesan bishops. If no bishop objects, the name of the nominee goes to all the Standing Committees of the several dioceses, and if a majority of those bodies approve, the Archbishop so informs the bishop-designate and asks the latter if he accepts or declines. It is interesting that the Archbishop, who is elected by the General Synod, is not attached to any one see as is the case in other Churches of the Anglican Communion.

The Province has no Prayer Book of its own, but is bound by its constitution to use the Book of Common Prayer of the Church of England with some allowed variations. Sixty per cent of the clergy are natives of New Zealand, and Anglicans make up some thirty-eight per cent of the total population.

The Far East

The Far East

THE HOLY CATHOLIC CHURCH IN CHINA
(CHUNG HUA SHENG KUNG HUI)

Buddhism arrived in China by way of India and gained a foothold in the first century of our era. But the majority of the Chinese until recent times were followers of Confucius, who died in 478 B.C. So far as early attempts to introduce Christianity are concerned, Nestorian Christians from Syria and Persia founded missions in China beginning in A.D. 657, while another attempt to introduce orthodox Christianity took place in the thirteenth century. In addition to these ventures, John of Montecorvino, a Franciscan friar, arrived at Peking at the beginning of the fourteenth century where he established a mission, but it was short-lived for the persecution of Christianity under the first Ming emperor stamped out both the Roman and Nestorian missions. After the lapse of another two and a half centuries, Jesuits, Dominicans, and Eastern Orthodox missionaries once again began the herculean task of rooting the Christian faith in China. The Roman Catholics had a real measure of success, so that by the end of the last century their adherents numbered over a million.

The Chinese Government, the East India Company, and the Roman Catholics succeeded in keeping other Christian groups out of China until well into the nineteenth century, for Robert Morrison, a Congregationalist, and the first western non-Roman missionary to China, had to travel by way of the United States in 1807 because the East India Company would not give him passage since he was a Protestant missionary. Later the Company employed Morrison as a translator, which meant that he had their protection while he published a Chinese dictionary and a Chinese version of the New Testament.

Beginning in 1733, the East India Company began shipping opium to China from India, in spite of the protests of the Chinese Government. This nefarious trade brought about the Anglo-Chinese War of 1839-42 which resulted in the Treaty of Nanking in the latter year, whereby the five treaty ports, Canton, Amoy, Foochow, Ningpo, and Shanghai, were opened to Western trade. By the terms of the Treaty missionaries were allowed to live in these ports for the first time, and Hong Kong was ceded to England. A second Anglo-Chinese war broke out in 1856 which resulted in the Treaty of Tientsin in 1858 and the Treaty of Peking in 1860. More ports were opened to the Westerners and the terms of the Treaty included toleration for western Christians and also for their Chinese converts. The interior of China was likewise opened to trade and missionary work at the same time.

Then began a period of vigorous missionary activity. The American Church had sent two clergymen out in 1835— Henry Lockwood and Francis Hanson. They went first to Canton, then to Batavia to learn Chinese and to begin a small school. William J. Boone, destined to become a notable name in China, joined the original two in 1837, and five years later when the Treaty Ports were opened, he went to Amoy to establish a permanent mission. By 1844 Boone was called home and consecrated "Missionary Bishop of Amoy and other parts of the Chinese Empire as the Board (of Missions) may hereafter designate." [24]

Boone was the real founder of the American Church's work in China. He soon moved to the newly-opened port of Shanghai at the mouth of the Yangtze-Kiang, perceiving that the latter could be the "highway of the Gospel" to the interior of China. This was to be the area in which the American Church worked over the years and which eventuated in the erection of the dioceses of Shanghai in 1901, and Anking and Hankow in 1910. Boone began a small school at Shanghai in 1846 which was destined in course of time to become one of the notable educational institutions of the Orient, St. John's University. Christ Church, Shanghai, was erected in 1851.

The Church of England sent missionaries to the southern coastal area, where in 1844 C.M.S. workers united with the S.P.G. missionaries who had arrived in Hong Kong the previous year. These two groups helped in the establishment of the first bishopric of Hong Kong in 1849, when George Smith was consecrated for that see. C.M.S. reached out from Hong Kong west to Kwantung and Kwangsi and northwest to Hunan; they also worked from Foochow to Fukien where they were assisted in time by the Dublin University Fukien Mission. This Mid-China Mission was highly successful for it became a diocese in 1880, and towards the end of the century the number of baptized Christians grew from 2,400 in 1892 to 5,900 in 1894.

The death of Bishop Boone in 1864 left the American Mission with a tiny staff of ten without a leader. The Civil War in the United States took Americans' minds off China so that financial support practically ceased. The American Church did its best by giving Bishop Channing Moore Williams, whom it had made Bishop of Japan in 1866, additional jurisdiction over China. Bishop Williams attended the first Lambeth Conference in 1867, so he did not arrive in China until the following year. But before he left, he succeeded in opening up work in Hankow and Wuchang, soon to be important centers of the American Mission. However, there were pressing problems in Japan, which was two thousand miles away, so Williams asked to be relieved of China in 1873.

The Church of England S.P.G. also began work in the north of China in 1863, but it was not until almost another decade had elapsed that a permanent mission was begun in Chefoo on the Yellow Sea east of Peking. Charles A. Russell became Bishop of North China in 1872 until the northern section was divided. In that same period Charles Perry Scott was consecrated for the six northern provinces in 1880, with headquarters at Peking. By 1895, W. W. Cassells became Bishop of Western Szechwan, so that the English dioceses now numbered four.

The American Church in 1877 consecrated, as Bishop for Shanghai, a man who ranks among the greatest of Anglicans—Samuel Isaac Joseph Schereschewsky,[25] a Lithuanian Jew who emigrated to the United States after studying in Germany and Poland. He had been attracted to Christianity while he was still in Europe, but after coming to America he was converted and baptized. He studied for Holy Orders, was ordained in 1859, and sailed immediately for China where he began his immensely important translations of the Bible and the Prayer Book. A master linguist, he spoke thirteen languages and read twenty. Upon his arrival, he spent nine hours a day learning Chinese. After his consecration in the United States and before sailing back to China, Schereschewsky raised $30,000 for a college to train Chinese youth "for the service of Christ," and on Easter Monday, 1879, the cornerstone of St. John's College, Shanghai, was laid. It had the Bishop and three other missionaries as the faculty. The fund grew to $52,000 by 1884, and a theological department was added for training a native ministry, together with medical and English departments.

Schereschewsky resigned in 1883, some time after the effects of a paralytic stroke failed to wear off. His mind continued to be as keen as ever, and he continued first in Shanghai, then in Tokyo, with his translations, which he accomplished by sitting in a chair and hitting the typewriter keys one at a time with a stick. He died in 1906, and was succeeded in Shanghai by W. J. Boone (1884-1901), and by Frederick Rogers Graves (1884-1937).

An important conference of the British and American missionaries was held in Shanghai in 1909 under the presidency of Bishop C. P. Scott of North China. It was the first representative assembly of the Anglicans in China, and it resulted in the meeting of a General Synod in 1912 when a constitution was adopted and the Church given the name: *Chung Hua Sheng Kung Hui*. It was recognized as an autonomous branch of the Anglican Communion by the Lambeth Conference of 1930. The Church now had thirteen dioceses, three of them of American origin, nine of English, and one, Honan, which was the special care of the Canadian Church.

The period from 1895 to 1930 was one of great opportunities for the Church. Until 1906 all of the modern education in the land was being given by mission schools and colleges, with the result that many Chinese leaders were products of these schools. Before World War II, there were thirteen

Christian universities and colleges operating in China with some 6,000 students, 300 middle schools with 50,000 students, and 4,000 primary schools with some 125,000 children. St. John's, Shanghai, also continued to progress, especially from 1888 to 1941, during which period it had as its distinguished head Dr. Francis L. H. Pott. Before World War II, ten per cent of all college men in China were St. John's graduates and of these, sixty per cent held responsible positions in government.

Boone College at Wuchang, named after China's first bishop, began as a middle school in 1871, and graduated its first college class in 1906. Incorporated as a university three years later, Boone became a major unit in the foundation of Central China College in 1924. During World War II, faculty and students moved to western Yunnan. Dispensaries made their appearance early as a necessary phase of Christian missionary concern. St. John's Medical School was begun, as we have seen, in 1880; while somewhat later St. Elizabeth's Hospital, Shanghai, and St. Andrew's Hospital, Wusih, expanded Christian medical missionary work in China.

The Boxer uprising in 1900 cost the lives of many missionaries and thousands of Chinese Christians were killed. As it turned out, the final suppression of the Boxers did not keep the shaky government in power for many more years, for the revolution brought about the fall of the Manchu dynasty and the birth of the Republic of China under the leader Sun Yat Sen. On his deathbed the latter said to a friend, "I want it known I die as a Christian," for he had been baptized in Hong Kong many years before.[26]

After 1920, Communism began to affect China. It became all the more powerful because of constant civil war by local war lords, high taxation, official corruption, and great poverty among the masses. By 1933 it was estimated that there were 75,000,000 Communists in China.

The years from 1937 to 1949 were harrowing ones. To begin with, there was the Japanese invasion of 1937. General Chiang Kai-shek tried desperately to unite China in the years before the invasion, but without success, due largely to the growing power of the Communists, the power of the local war lords, and the inaction of the West. When William Payne Roberts was consecrated the seventh Bishop of Shanghai in November, 1937, two-thirds of his diocese was in physical ruins and the remaining third dangerously vulnerable to the Japanese armies. Nanking became a holocaust the next month. Eighteen missionaries stayed at their posts while the Japanese killed twenty thousand civilians.

The war against Japan, starting in December, 1941, brought the United States and the British Commonwealth to China's aid via the Burma Road, which connected with Chiang Kai-shek's new capital, Chungking. The years from 1941 to 1948 saw an era of good feeling between the Western Allies and Free China. Missionaries were welcomed and the Free Government subsidized Christian colleges and hospitals. Central China College had been moved from Hankow to Hsichow in 1942, as were the Church's secondary schools. In those years it is estimated that there were almost three quarters of a million adult non-Roman Christians in China, while in the Anglican Church, the Chinese clergy and teachers far outnumbered the Westerners. Chinese assistant bishops were elected and consecrated for Hong Kong and Anking in 1940, and for Shanghai in 1942, but because of the troubled times there could be no meeting of the General Synod in the decade 1937-1947. Nevertheless, every

169

diocese had its own synod and some of them were able to meet in spite of the difficulties.

The fourteen dioceses prior to 1949 bore strong marks of their national and ecclesiastical origin. Fukien, Chekiang, Kwangsi, Hunan, Western Szechwan, and Hong Kong were the spiritual children of C.M.S.; North China and Shantung were heirs of S.P.G.; the American Church had the responsibility of Hankow, Anking, and Shanghai; and the Canadian Church had Honan. The one missionary district of Shensi had been the responsibility of the whole Chinese Church, by its own desire, since 1916.

With the Japanese surrender on September 2, 1945, China was free again, only to be plunged once more into war between the Nationalists and the Communists. The latter were successful in the struggle, and the Generalissimo retreated to Formosa. The Communist People's Government of China was set up on October 1, 1949, and the disciplined behavior of the Communist armies did much to win for the new government the sympathy of the civil population. At this time eight of the fourteen bishops of the Chinese Church were Americans, and the leadership of the non-Roman Christians was still largely in the hands of Westerners. The attitude of the government slowly hardened towards these Westerners, so that in the course of the next three years the number of Western missionaries in China was reduced from six thousand to two thousand, while more than a hundred Chinese and "foreign" Christians were executed and many more imprisoned and persecuted. In December, 1950, the entire American staff of the Chinese Church were ordered home since their very presence was a danger to Chinese Christians. Bishop Roberts was the last to leave.

The non-Roman seminaries, as well as the educational

and medical institutions, were merged by order of the Government so that the Yenching Theological Seminary, founded in April, 1953, now serves seven denominations including the Anglicans. The Nanking Seminary, founded the following year, has fifteen denominations; the Anglicans have their own chapel, and the total enrollment is over one hundred.

The government did not allow any representatives of the Church in China to attend the Anglican Congress in 1954, but restrictions have apparently been lessened since because Bishop K. H. Ting of Chekiang attended a meeting of the Central Committee of the World Council of Churches in Hungary, and a meeting of the Consultative Committee of the Lambeth Conference in England in the summer of 1956. It is to be hoped that the Chinese Church will be represented at the Lambeth Conference of 1958. Bishop Ting reported that there is no state interference with religion in China and that he had, in his small diocese, confirmed six hundred and seventy people in November, 1955. Bishop Ronald Hall of Hong Kong also reported that in a recent visit to the mainland he found "religious freedom and a growing Church." [27]

The House of Bishops which met in Shanghai in May, 1956, issued a Pastoral Letter which stressed the present complete independence of the Church, its entire self-support, and the increasing cooperation between the dioceses. There are at present fourteen dioceses and seventeen bishops, all of them Chinese, with the Right Reverend Robin Chen as the Presiding Bishop. The Diocese of Victoria, Hong Kong, enjoys a peculiar status in that it was transferred to the jurisdiction of the Archbishop of Canterbury.

A draft Prayer Book has been completed recently, and

when it is published the Church will have one Prayer Book for the first time in its history. Before that time some dioceses used the Church of England Prayer Book, and others the American Book of Common Prayer.

As the years add perspective, and the century of Western Christian missionary activity in China from 1844 to 1949 are better understood, Chinese Christians may be expected to understand that with all its faults the Church did bring the Gospel to China, and that it led the attacks against the opium trade, the killing of infant daughters, concubinage, and foot-binding, all of which, with other evils, were part of China's former life.

THE HOLY CATHOLIC CHURCH IN JAPAN (NIPPON SEI KO KWAI)

For almost two and a half centuries before the opening of Japan in 1853, the Islands had been closed to the rest of the world. The result of this isolation has been that, during the past century, the Japanese have had to evolve from a feudal type of government to a modern industrial society. From A.D. 784, and for the following six and a half centuries, the Emperor was regarded as the divine head of the State. The real power was later held by the Shoguns. Until 1868 they occupied a position in Japan similar to that of the Mayors of the Palace in the time of the Frankish Merovingian kings. Local control was in the hands of Daimyon who resembled the feudal nobles of medieval days.

Intrepid navigators from Portugal, Spain, and Holland reached Japan in the sixteenth century and opened up trade; and about the same time St. Francis Xavier heard of Japan when he went over to Malacca from India. Xavier landed at Kagoshima in 1549 and founded a mission there with his

172

companions. It was so successful that by 1582 there were 150,000 Christians; and by the end of the century the number had increased to 250,000.

By 1614 the sixty-five years of work had crashed into ruins when the dictator Hideyoshi ordered the Christian faith proscribed, its adherents slain, and its priests killed and banished. With the exception of a few Dutch who were allowed to remain under humiliating conditions, all Europeans were driven out, and for the following two and a half centuries Japan remained closed to the West. The persecution of Christians continued, culminating in a massacre at Shimbara where 37,000 faithful perished at one time. It is thought that 250,000 Christians lost their lives between 1582 and 1614.

The government promulgated an edict of perpetual proscription of Christianity, an edict which remained in effect until the fourth quarter of the nineteenth century. In summing up this initial attempt to found the Christian faith in Japan a noted modern missionary has said, "Sixteenth century European Christianity was neither morally nor intellectually qualified for the task" of preaching Christ to Japan.[28] In spite of the long-term persecution, Christianity survived in Japan down to the middle of the nineteenth century when Perry paid his famous visit.

During the time of their isolation the Japanese developed their internal resources, including religion, with the result that the period saw a rapid growth of Shinto and Emperor worship for the middle and lower classes, while the intellectuals tended to study Confucianism. This explains in large part the remarkable degree of resistance to Christianity when it was reintroduced in the middle of the nineteenth century.

Following the opening of Japan by Commodore Perry in 1853, a treaty was negotiated between Japan and the United

States which opened up certain ports to Western trade; succeeding treaties made it possible for missionaries to worship as they pleased and to build churches. No permission was given to evangelize the Japanese; indeed, active persecution of Christians continued until 1872. And it was not until 1890 that most of the hindrances to evangelization were removed.

The American Church decided to begin work in Japan with a staff of two clergy. One of them, John Liggins, was already in Nagasaki recuperating from his tour of duty in China; the other, Channing Moore Williams, arrived in Nagasaki via Rio de Janeiro, Sydney and Shanghai, in June of 1858, seven months after leaving New York. The young clergyman, not yet thirty, was destined to spend the next fifty years of his life in Japan and to have an important part in laying the foundations of the Japanese Church. Williams and Liggins found signboards everywhere which read: "Nobody is permitted to believe in Christianity, the evil religion." This was no idle warning, for nationals might be executed if they embraced the Christian faith, while the new missionaries suffered actual persecution. The mission went with discouraging slowness in those early years, and Williams found himself writing to the Mission Board in 1864: "Our hope to preach the Gospel in Japan publicly has not been fulfilled yet. What we have done, and are going to do, is to act as spiritual farmers, so to speak, removing stones from the fields and cutting hay." [29] The public notice boards displaying the edict against Christianity were not all removed until 1873.

Williams had built the first non-Roman church in Nagasaki in 1862, but not until four years later was the first Japanese converted and baptized. This was the same year, 1866, that Williams was called home to be consecrated first bishop in Japan, with additional jurisdiction over China. After his

174

consecration, Williams attended the first Lambeth Conference in 1867, and then made a visitation to China, so he did not get back to Japan until 1868. A political revolution took place in Japan that same year which resulted in the restoration of the theocratic state. The landed aristocracy and the newly-rich seized control of the new economy of production; and while the Emperor still remained as the object of worship, the real rulers were the army and navy and the new plutocracy.

The same year that C.M.S. began work in Nagasaki, 1869, Bishop Williams decided to transfer his headquarters to Osaka, where he remained for four years until he made the move to Tokyo in 1873; the latter city had become the new capital of Japan and was therefore a more strategic center for the Church. It was during this period that the Bishop founded a school which later became St. Paul's University, and also a small hospital. In 1873 S.P.G. sent its first mission to Japan; so there were now three Anglican groups at work, all quite independent of one another. The two Church of England societies, C.M.S. and S.P.G., worked in those areas which now comprise the dioceses of Hokkaido, South Tokyo, Kobe, and Kyushu; the Americans in what is now Tohuku, North Kanto, and Kyoto. The Canadian Church had entered the field in 1888, and by 1912 they took over the diocese of Mid-Japan which was separated from Osaka. Because the work had grown up over the years without any central authority, the total situation was very confused and there were no diocesan boundaries. This meant that various converts were under the jurisdiction of their Bishop, English or American, irrespective of where they lived. Thus Bishop Bickersteth, who replaced the first English Bishop Poole in 1886, was obliged to cover the whole of Japan and Okinawa as well! The American

Bishop was under a somewhat similar handicap, so it was obvious that action should be taken.

By the time Bickersteth reached Japan, Williams had been a bishop there for almost a quarter of a century. It was fortunate that his strong, sound, missionary record was complemented by Bickersteth's experience as head of the Cambridge University Mission to Delhi, coupled with his brilliant mind and devout spirit. It was under the wise guidance of the two bishops that united conferences were held between the three Anglican groups which culminated in a General Synod held at Osaka in 1887 where a Constitution and Canons were adopted by the delegates and Nippon Sei Ko Kwai was born. They also organized a Missionary Society. As Bishop Bickersteth rightly said of this event: "The organization of this body is of more than local significance inasmuch as it is the first instance of the foundation of a fully organized and autonomous Church in the near or far East in modern times." This primary Synod was attended by the two bishops, eighteen missionaries, and fifty-two Japanese, three of whom were deacons. Several years before this the Anglican groups had agreed to use a common Prayer Book, and a translation of this had been effected by 1878.

Slow but steady progress had been made up to 1887, for there were now some twelve hundred Japanese Anglicans of twenty churches in Tokyo, Osaka, Kumamoto, and Hakodate. It was unfortunate that the American Church allowed four years to elapse before Bishop Williams' successor, John Cole McKim, arrived; but the General Synods of 1894 and 1896 succeeded in largely eliminating the overlapping "spheres of influence," and six missionary districts were formally recognized. Later the six became ten.

Educational, hospital, and social service work were especially emphasized. Bickersteth began St. Andrew's University Mission to men and boys in Tokyo almost as soon as he arrived. It was modelled on similar lines to the Universities' Mission to Delhi of which he had been the head some years before. The educational mission in Tokyo was staffed by Oxford and Cambridge men. He also began a similar community mission for women, called St. Hilda's. The Americans had a school for girls, St. Margaret's, at Osaka, begun in 1875. The famous St. Paul's University, Tokyo, was begun in 1907; it was the outgrowth of an earlier institution started by Bishop Williams. Also under the American Church was St. Barnabas Hospital in Kyoto, begun as a dispensary in 1874, to which Dr. Henry Laning gave forty years of unremitting effort. The most notable American hospital was St. Luke's, Tokyo, which had also begun as a small dispensary in 1891. That gave way to a twenty-three bed hospital in 1902, while seven years later the institution had grown into a general hospital with ninety beds. In 1912 plans were laid for a new hospital over twice the size of the former building, but the foundations were destroyed by the earthquake and fire of 1923. The hospital's heroic director, Dr. Rudolph Bolling Teusler, was still undismayed for he immediately set about raising money for a new and larger hospital which was subsequently erected. Teusler died in 1934, the year after the new St. Luke's was completed. Miraculously, the structure escaped the bombings of World War II, and in 1945 it was taken over by the American Army of Occupation. Recently it was returned to the Church.

A notable work among lepers was begun in 1895 by an Englishwoman, Miss Hannah Riddell at Kumamoto; and another leper work opened at Kasatsu in 1911 under the direction of Miss Mary Cornwall-Legh. Perhaps the most famous piece of mission work in the then appalling slums of Tokyo was accomplished by the Reverend Yosimichi Sigiura who worked there for forty years, beginning in 1876.

As the nineteenth century drew to a close, the Japanese government grew increasingly nationalistic and planned to direct all educational activity. By 1889 the Board of Education ruled that no religious education might be given, nor might religious ceremonies be performed, in Christian schools. When Japan defeated Russia in 1904, she became more convinced that her manifest destiny was to rule the Orient and that Western invincibility was a myth.

More Japanese were ordained during these years so that by the time of the General Synod of 1923 there was a majority of Japanese in both the clerical and lay orders; this was in striking contrast to the primary Synod of 1887 where the nationals were a small minority. Also, at the Synod of 1923 the Dioceses of Tokyo and Osaka were erected and two Japanese clergy were consecrated for those sees. By 1940 the Church had 23,000 members and more than two hundred Japanese clergy.

In 1939 and 1941 the government took two further steps in the control of religion, for in the former year the Religions Bill made Shinto, Buddhism, and Christianity the three recognized religions of Japan; while in 1941 the Religious Organizations Law barred foreigners from holding any office of authority in any church, and forbade churches receiving any financial aid from abroad. Accordingly, the foreign bishops and leaders went home, leaving the Church to the direction of the Japanese bishops now ten in number. The American and British Churches sent money, before the deadline, to help in the emergency.

Early in the war the government proceeded to order all Protestant Churches to dissolve and merge into a Japan United Church, a measure which caused great distress and debate within the Nippon Sei Ko Kwai. Finally, the Presiding Bishop, Naida, with his diocese of Osaka, and two other bishops, Yanagihara and Matsui, joined the United Church, and some sixty-eight Anglican congregations out of the total two hundred and thirty-two conformed to the government's edict and joined the new Church. The remainder, led by Bishop Yashiro, remained faithful and suffered varying degrees of imprisonment and persecution from 1942 until the end of the war.

When the war ended, the Church had to face many serious problems. The bombings had destroyed some eighty churches and four schools, and only four out of twenty-five churches were left standing in Tokyo. Added to this was the schism of the war years, which was complicated by the fact that the three seceding bishops had consecrated seven other bishops during the war. The situation was in some ways parallel to that which faced the first General Convention of the Church in the United States after the Civil War was over. It is good to record that charity and good will prevailed in the Japanese Church. The bishops and congregations were received back into the Nippon Sei Ko Kwai, and the schism ended.

The first General Synod of the post-war period met at St. Paul's University, Tokyo, in 1946, when the Church was reincorporated with its original Constitution and Canons; it took the sound point of view that the government wartime edict demanding its dissolution was null and void. It also set up a new National Council and staff to implement its decisions. Bishop Yashiro, the Presiding Bishop, emerges as the hero of the war period in holding the Church together, in suffering persecution, and in setting the strategy for the post-war opportunities.

After the war, representatives went to Japan from England, Canada, and the United States, both to assist in the reconciliation and to help the Church get back on its feet. Because of the paramount need for clergy and for rebuilding, a special grant of seventy thousand pounds was made over a period of years for the salaries of professors in the theological college and for the reconstruction of churches. The Central Theological College had not functioned during the war, but a new site was chosen and new buildings begun in 1952. The second General Synod of the post-war period was held in 1953 at Tokyo; among other things it gave approval for the use of a revised Communion Service during the following triennium. This revision has been greatly influenced by the South African Liturgy. Many thousands of churchmen were killed during the hostilities and many thousands more were dispersed from the cities, where Anglicans were strongest, to the villages where there were few churches of their communion. As a consequence the total membership declined in the post-war years.

The Diocese of Tokyo contains a number of Church institutions, among them Central Theological College, St. Luke's Hospital, and St. Paul's University with its schools. In South Tokyo, the Brotherhood of St. Andrew sponsors a notable educational project, and North Kanto has St. Barnabas' Mission to lepers. In all the Church has forty-two colleges, schools, hospitals, orphanages, and special social service projects. The schools have some 16,000 pupils attending them.

There has been a lack of spontaneous growth since the war, which is disturbing but understandable. The Church needs a mobile strategy for advance, particularly in the country regions, and there is great and continuing need for non-dominating assistance and understanding from the West.

There are ten dioceses at present and these are now drawing closer to one another because of the decline in influence of the various missionary societies. There is a likelihood that an Archbishop will soon be chosen for the Japanese Church. It is interesting that in Japan today there is no open hostility to Christianity as there is in other parts of the Far East, although the greatest percentage of Japanese are at present atheists. Up to the present very few laborers and very few farmers are Christians, which indicates the pressing need for working with these groups.

The Japanese Church conducts missionary work in Okinawa jointly with the American Church, and this work is under the direction of the Bishop of Honolulu.

THE DIOCESE OF KOREA
(CHOSEN SUNG KUNG WHAI)

The peninsula which is Korea is strangely like Florida in its shape, but is half as large again as the latter. It is the home of a race that is neither Japanese nor Chinese, whose religion was almost totally Buddhist for the millennium between 392 and 1392; and Buddhist influence has continued to the present. While Confucianism has been widespread amongst the upper classes until recent years, the great bulk of the people have worshipped evil spirits.

Jesuit priests reached the "Land of Morning Calm" in the eighteenth century, but the severe persecution of Christians and a general anti-western attitude among the populace made missionary work extremely difficult. Christianity was a prohibited religion through the first half of the nineteenth

181

century, and even after the treaty between the United States and Korea in 1882, missionaries and foreigners enjoyed only a restricted right of residence in Seoul and the three recently opened treaty ports. They could not travel inland, except for trade or pleasure, on pain of deportation.

Although two Chinese Christians had settled on the southeast coast in 1885, it was the Archbishop of Canterbury who initiated organized work by asking Bishop Scott of North China and Bishop Bickersteth of Japan to visit Korea in 1887 and report to him the prospects for opening work there. As a result of this visit the Archbishop consecrated Charles John Corfe, a former Navy chaplain, as the first Bishop of Korea in 1889. The new bishop likened his task to "attacking a battleship with a dinghy." S.P.G. supplied funds, and within a decade the Bishop had five priests together with some medical work which brought encouraging results. However, the Bishop had to wait seven years before securing his first convert, and it was not until the time of his successor that the diocese came to be regarded as part of the total responsibility of the Anglican Church.

Japan annexed Korea in 1910 as part of the Japanese Empire, and to forestall the Russians who were still busy finishing their trans-Siberian railroad. This brought up the question as to whether the diocese of Korea should be annexed to Nippon Sei Ko Kwai, but the then Bishop Mark N. Trollope was against it for he wished to see Korea organized as a separate province with three distinct dioceses. Attempts were made to carry this through in 1922 and 1925, and an assistant bishop was consecrated with this in mind in 1926, but Trollope's death in 1930, and other complications, caused the plan to fall through.

A great deal was done, nevertheless, during the nineteen

years of Trollope's episcopate. He was an outstanding scholar and mastered both Korean and Japanese, and he was able to organize the Church into a workable Synod with a Constitution. Prior to World War II, St. Michael's Theological College at Chemulpo trained a number of nationals for the priesthood; indeed, the first Korean priest had been ordained as far back as 1911. A great deal of evangelistic work was done in the northern villages with the result that mass movements to Christianity began to take place. These never reached fruition because the Japanese made a planned effort to destroy the Christian faith in Korea from 1936 to 1945.

The collapse of Japan after World War II caused Korea to regain her independence for a short time; but very soon Communist infiltration from the north caused trouble ending with the partition of Korea and then the Korean War. Bishop Cecil Cooper, who had been a missionary in Korea since 1908, was consecrated its Bishop in 1930. Despite his best efforts the Church was sadly diminished and almost extinguished during the war, when the Bishop and his clergy suffered imprisonment and untold hardship.

The Diocese is still a missionary jurisdiction under the Archbishop of Canterbury; its Prayer Book reached its final form in 1935 and is, in general, a translation of the 1549 book.

THE PHILIPPINE EPISCOPAL CHURCH

The intrepid explorer Magellan discovered the Philippines in 1521 on his first journey around the world; but he did not live long afterwards for he was killed during a quarrel on the Island of Cebu. Forty years later, Legazpi, with an army of occupation, annexed the islands in the name of his sovereign, Philip II of Spain. The Philippines are heterogeneous both physically and racially. They comprise 7,000 islands, of which about 3,000 are habitable, and there are twenty million inhabitants spread over some 115,000 square miles. More than twenty racial groups are accounted for in this total, and they speak eight distinct languages and more than eighty dialects.

As the nineteenth century drew to a close, the Filipinos revolted against the harsh Spanish rule and organized a republic. The Islands then came under the military protection of the United States, for which privilege the latter paid Spain twenty million dollars. The military rule of the United States ended shortly, and the first civil governor, Mr. William Howard Taft, was appointed in 1901.

The American Church, realizing its spiritual responsibilities in the new area, appointed the Bishop of Shanghai, Frederick Rogers Graves, to take oversight of Manila, and he made an episcopal visitation in September of 1898. It is interesting that no church other than the Roman Catholic had been allowed in the Philippines until this time, but now the ecclesiastical monopoly was broken.

The American Church took a momentous step when it elected the thirty-nine-year-old rector of St. Stephen's Church in Boston as the first missionary Bishop of the Philippines in 1901. Charles Henry Brent left for his new work the next summer, sailed on the same ship with Mr. Taft, and began work immediately in Manila where he established a church, and shortly thereafter a hospital (St. Luke's) and a school. Discovering that there were more than 30,000 Chinese in Manila, Brent began a church and a school for them in 1905, a work that has had great success over the years. Today St. Stephen's Chinese School has 1,500 pupils.

Brent's next move was north and west on the Island of

Luzon. He made his initial visitation of that area by horse and mule back, wagon, launch, and on foot; here he encountered the head-hunting Igorots, whose lives were tyrannized by the fear of evil spirits. Brent began missions at three places on Luzon: at Bontoc in 1903, Sagada in 1904, and Besao in 1910; he also began schools for the native children. A small church was built at Baguio by 1906, together with Easter School, and it is told that six boys who attended the latter in its earliest days came from Bontoc and walked a hundred miles across the mountains to get there. Later on high schools were built in Sagada and Balbalasang, and also a hospital in the former place. The work showed steady progress. Although a native ministry was slow in developing, two Igorots were ordained just before World War II, and it was they who did much to carry on the Church's work in that area during the terrible days that followed.

The second area which Brent opened for mission work was on the southern island of Mindanao where the Moros lived. These Moslems were a constant challenge to Brent who felt that they offered the Christian missionary a unique opportunity to demonstrate the power of the Gospel. The Moros, apparently untamable, were pirates by occupation, and they had successfully resisted any efforts of the Spanish Government to bring them under its authority. Brent opened a school for Moro boys at Jolo. This met with notable success, thanks to the efforts of Mrs. Lorillard Spencer, who lived at Jolo and did much for the school.

A church was built in Zamboanga by 1905, and a dispensary was erected to minister to the physical needs of the Moro people; later it became Brent Hospital, an institution which performed great service until its destruction in World War II. A new hospital was erected and dedicated in 1953. The

185

work of the Church with the Moros has continued, but progress is slow as always with Moslems where advances must be measured by decades rather than years. A further station was opened in another section of Mindanao, at Upi in 1923, and a church building followed some years later. Brent's episcopate in the Philippines was made more difficult not only by insufficient funds and personnel, which are problems that attend all missionary bishops, but by his many absences from the diocese.

Some years before World War I Brent had become an international figure. He was president of the First International Conference on Opium at Shanghai in 1909, and he presided also at a second and similar Conference at The Hague in 1911. Between these two events Brent attended the International Missionary Conference at Edinburgh where he became a zealous convert to the ecumenical movement; and from that time onwards he gave himself unremittingly to that cause. He was the president of the First World Conference on Faith and Order at Lausanne in 1927. Brent resigned from the Philippines in 1918 to become Bishop of Western New York, and Gouverneur Frank Mosher took his place.

Mosher proved to be an excellent choice after Brent, for the new Bishop concentrated on his diocese, and was able, through his gifts of wise administration, to consolidate and also carry forward the pioneer work of his predecessor.

Upon Mosher's death, Norman Binsted was translated from the Diocese of Sendai in Japan to be the third Bishop of the Philippines. He went to his new post shortly before the outbreak of the war between the United States and Japan. Binsted's new diocese was soon to be in physical ruins, for during the Japanese occupation churches were either destroyed or occupied, many Christians were killed or scattered, and the new

Bishop with many of his clergy were interned and suffered great hardship.

In keeping with the widespread desire of Oriental peoples to be independent of Western powers, the United States Government had passed an Act in 1934 providing for complete independence for the Philippines ten years from that date. The fulfillment of the promise was delayed somewhat by the war, but independence did come on July 4, 1946. It was a most significant day for developing good relations between the Islands and the United States.

The Episcopal Church in the Philippines has been fortunate to have two really great men as bishops in a little over half a century, Brent and Binsted. There was need for vision, courage, and wisdom, all of which they both possessed. The Japanese defense of Manila in the last days of the war meant, among other things, that the Cathedral and other properties of the Church in the capital were entirely destroyed. Rebuilding has been made possible through the purchase of a thirty-six acre site outside Manila where a new Cathedral, a new St. Luke's Hospital, and a new St. Andrew's Theological Seminary have been erected, together with other buildings. The seminary had been founded in 1937 for training Filipino clergy, but it was hardly started before the war came, and the faculty was interned and the students dispersed. There is currently a full faculty and over forty men enrolled, half of whom are members of the Philippine Independent Church. Back of all this was the untiring energy of the Bishop.

The far-seeing statesmanship of Bishop Binsted is notably illustrated in his negotiations with the problem, and opportunity, presented by the Philippine Independent Church. The history of the latter goes back to a revolt in 1898 against abuses, both ecclesiastical and political, of the Spanish Government. Certain leading Roman Catholics appealed to the Pope to end these abuses, but nothing came of the appeal, probably because the Pope was disinclined to annoy Spain. Incensed at the neglect of their legitimate grievances, a large number of former Roman Catholics with some one hundred clergy left the Roman fold and founded the Philippine Independent Church in 1902. The Roman Church brought suit against them in 1906, in consequence of which they lost all their church property, a circumstance which dismayed but did not daunt them.

Monsignor Gregorio Aglipay, the former Vicar-General of the Republic and now the head of the new Church, asked both Bishop Brent and the Old Catholic bishops for valid orders, but nothing was done. As a consequence the Church drifted towards Unitarianism and a large section of the seceders returned to Rome. Had Brent seized this opportunity, he could have done a very great deal for Christian reunion even before the Edinburgh Conference. After the war, in 1947, a theological reversal took place and the Church under Bishop de los Reyes made a declaration of its intention henceforth to believe and to teach the orthodox and Catholic faith. Negotiations were opened with Bishop Binsted with the consequence that he, together with two other American bishops, consecrated three clergy of the Independent Church including their Supreme Bishop, de los Reyes, as bishops of the Church of God. This historic event took place in 1948, with the result that almost two million Filipinos are now closely allied with the Episcopal Church and the Anglican Communion. For several years the Independent clergy have received training at St. Andrew's Seminary.

The Episcopal Church in the Philippines is not a province of the Anglican Communion due to the fact that it comprises but one diocese, and is still, strictly speaking, a missionary district of the American Church. In view of its growing relationship with the Philippine Independent Church, the future of the American work would seem to be in an ultimate merger of the two Churches and the subsequent erection of several dioceses to form a new province in communion with the See of Canterbury.

THE MISSIONARY DISTRICT
OF HONOLULU

In spite of many appeals for missionaries to the Hawaiians, the Church of England sent no one until 1861, eighty-three years after Captain Cook had landed there and named the islands after his financial backer, the Earl of Sandwich. Finally, the missionaries came after Queen Emma had made a personal appeal to Queen Victoria. There were plans afoot at that time for a joint missionary venture by the Church of England and the Episcopal Church, but the Civil War caused the plans to be abandoned, and Thomas Staley was consecrated for the Islands in 1861, where he served until 1870. It was a year later that Henry Benjamin Whipple, Bishop of Minnesota, was offered the bishopric of the Sandwich Islands, so that he might "lay the foundations which shall extend throughout those Islands until you meet Bishop Patteson from the South." [30] Whipple was flattered, perhaps tempted, but he felt obliged to decline. Perhaps it was just as well, for Staley's successor, Alfred Willis, not only spent thirty years as second Bishop of the Islands, but after he resigned at the age of sixty-five, he spent eighteen more years as first missionary bishop of the Tonga and Friendly Islands.

By 1871 both Chinese and Japanese were beginning to arrive on the Islands in large numbers, but it was a challenge

189

to which the Church was somewhat slow to respond. Hawaii was assuming greater strategic importance as the years went by, and in 1884 the United States leased Pearl Harbor as a naval station to forestall Japan, and finally annexed the Islands in 1898. Full territorial status was given to Hawaii in 1900.

After over forty years of work there, the Church of England finally transferred jurisdiction to the Episcopal Church in 1902, since it was obvious that the American Church had both the resources and the interest in the work. St. Andrew's Priory School for Girls and Iolani School for Boys, both in Honolulu, are doing valuable work for children of all races, and are both outstanding institutions.

In 1944, Harry S. Kennedy became the sixth bishop. During his episcopate Guam, Midway, Wake, Okinawa, and Formosa (Taiwan) have been added to the jurisdiction. In 1951 work in Okinawa began jointly with the Japanese Church, which supplies one half of the clergy, while missionary work was begun in Taiwan by the American Church in 1952.

CHAPTER SEVEN

Europe and the Near East

Europe and the Near East

ANGLICAN WORK IN EUROPE

North and Central Europe. This is not a diocese but an "extra-diocesan jurisdiction of the Bishop of London, exercised on his behalf by the Bishop of Fulham, a suffragan of London." The Bishop visits some thirty chaplaincies in the major cities of North and Central Europe from Moscow to Berlin, the Scandinavian capitals, Brussels, The Hague and Paris. He also visits personnel of the British Armed Forces stationed in various parts of North and Central Europe.

Organized work on the Continent began as early as 1699, and three years later a church was built for the British colony in Amsterdam. In 1703 S.P.G. provided the salary of a chaplain for Moscow together with Greek liturgies. An important aspect of the work is the establishment and continuation of friendly contact with the Orthodox, the Old Catholics, and the Lutherans in the area. The present jurisdiction was founded in 1911.

The Diocese of Gibraltar, a diocese under the jurisdiction of the Archbishop of Canterbury. The diocese was founded in 1842 for the primary purpose of ministering to British residents in the Mediterranean. The area embraced in the vast jurisdiction is approximately the same as that of the Roman Empire except for North Africa, Palestine and Cyprus. Besides Gibraltar the Bishop visits chaplaincies in Spain, Portugal, Madeira, Italy, and Greece, the seaboard islands of the Mediterranean, the Black and Caspian Seas, the Adriatic and Greek archipelagos, Turkey, Roumania, Bulgaria, Yugoslavia, Albania, Southern Russia, and Asia Minor.

The capture of Gibraltar by the British in 1704, the Empire's rapid development in the Far East, and the opening of the Suez Canal in 1869, required many Church of England members in government and civil service to live in the countries around the Mediterranean, and the shepherding of the scattered flock was the reason for the establishment of the Diocese.

There are at present some sixty-five churches in the large area, and many chaplaincies, so it involves incessant travelling on the part of the diocesan. Of particular importance is the Church's relationship with the Orthodox clergy and people. There is a Cathedral at Gibraltar and a fine Collegiate Church at Malta built by Queen Adelaide, the widow of William IV.

Convocation of American Churches in Europe. This Convocation consists of American churches in Paris, Frankfurt, Munich, Geneva, Nice, Florence, and Rome; there are also institutions connected with some of these. The Presiding Bishop appoints a bishop to have the supervision of the churches, and also to visit the Episcopal chaplains and personnel of the Armed Forces of the United States in the area.

THE ARCHBISHOPRIC IN JERUSALEM

Jerusalem is a Missionary Jurisdiction under the Archbishop of Canterbury, and its Archbishop is styled the Archbishop *in* and not *of* Jerusalem. He also has jurisdiction over the diocese of "Jordan, Syria, and Lebanon" as well as

194

Anglican congregations in Libya, Iraq, Israel, and Cyprus, together with the dioceses of Egypt, the Sudan, and Iran.

The Bishopric has a curious history, for it began in 1841 with the "Jerusalem Bishoprics Act" whereby the English Archbishops and Bishops were to consecrate a bishop for Jerusalem by a joint agreement between the Church of England and the Lutheran State Church of Prussia. The English Crown and the Prussian Crown were to nominate bishops alternatively. Michael Alexander, a Christian Jew, became the first Bishop in Jerusalem, that city then being in the Turkish Empire. Samuel Gobat, a nominee of the Prussian King, succeeded Alexander; but so much trouble developed that, after his episcopate, the Germans withdrew, leaving the Bishopric in the hands of the Church of England.

There is a very definite understanding that Anglicans do not attempt to convert the Orthodox and as a result friendly relations have been built up over the years. When the Bishopric was established it was stated in the Charter that it in no way entrenched upon the spiritual rights and liberties of the ancient Churches of the East. The Bishopric lapsed for some years between 1881 and 1887, after which a statement was issued by the English Archbishops and the Bishop of London which said, "The Bishop is to establish and maintain, as far as in him lies, relations of Christian charity with the other Churches represented in Jerusalem and especially with the Orthodox Church." [31] The work is financed largely by the "Jerusalem and the East Mission" founded in 1887. The Archbishop in Jerusalem is the representative of the whole Anglican Church in the Holy City, and takes his place with prelates of the Latin, Orthodox, Armenian, Syrian, Coptic, and Abyssinian Churches. There are great difficulties to be surmounted in working on both sides of the borders between Israel and Jordan; and this, together with problems raised by Arab Anglicans and the general tension in that area, calls for Christian statesmanship of the highest order.

The work centers at the Cathedral, or more properly the Collegiate Church of St. George in Jerusalem. Since 1954 the work of the diocese has received the support of the entire Anglican Communion. In 1957 the bishop in Jerusalem became an archbishop. In addition to oversight of the dioceses of Egypt, the Sudan and Iran, the new archbishop will supervise the creation of a new Bishopric of Jordan, Syria and the Lebanon. An Arab priest was consecrated first Bishop of this diocese in December 1957.

THE MISSIONARY DIOCESE OF IRAN

The Diocese of Iran was founded as the Diocese of Persia in 1912, but the name was changed in 1935 when the state assumed the name of Iran. Since World War I the government has passed from the hands of local *mullahs* and priests to a vigorous national government. It is a country predominantly Moslem where the Anglican Church claims a tiny fraction of the population of nineteen and a half millions.

This is the land where Henry Martyn labored so brilliantly but briefly at the beginning of the nineteenth century, and it was his example which inspired two nineteenth century Anglican bishops to resign their respective sees and devote the remainder of their lives to missionary work in Persia. Thomas Valmy French, formerly Bishop of Lahore, died at Muscat in 1891; and Bishop E. C. Stuart of Waiapu left New Zealand in 1896 to become a missionary to the Persians.

The first synod of the diocese was held in 1936 by the

Bishop and his three Iranian and seven European clergy, and it was followed by a series of missions which brought encouraging results. Since World War II disputes over oil led to the temporary expulsion of the Bishop. There have been various other hindrances besides nationalism. Work among Moslems is necessarily slow for it demands special training, and the results are not likely to be spectacular. The heart of the diocese is at Isfahan where there is a C.M.S. hospital which was erected in 1900; there is also another C.M.S. hospital in Shiraz.

CHAPTER EIGHT

The Faith and the Future
of the Anglican Communion

The Faith and the Future of the Anglican Communion

The Churches of the Anglican Communion are committed to believe and to teach the Catholic faith once delivered to the saints, a faith purged of medieval superstition and errors, which gives adequate attention to tradition but does not equate tradition with The Tradition of the New Testament. The Anglican Church makes no claim to be the only true Church—indeed it comprises but five per cent of Christendom—but it does claim to be a part of the true Catholic Church founded by Jesus Christ. Likewise, Anglicans make no claim to infallibility, for history clearly reveals that Popes and General Councils, Bishops and Conventions have not seldom erred from the Faith. Anglicans simply believe that the Holy Spirit is in the Church as Christ promised He would be, and that while He does inspire His Church and lead it into all truth, there can be no guarantee of perpetual infallibility for any one or for all of its members.

Every one of the provinces and dioceses which comprise the Anglican Communion has inherited from the Mother Church of England certain general characteristics which are the common marks of Anglicanism. One striking feature of the Anglican Church is a remarkable inclusiveness, which holds together a wide variety of Christians who emphasize varying facets of the Faith. Any lesser degree of inclusiveness would do violence to many legitimate expressions of historic Catholic religion, and any greater degree of inclusiveness would take Anglicans outside the historic faith. Another note is the insistence that the Holy Scriptures contain all things as generally necessary for salvation, and that the Church is committed to teach nothing as essential for the same that cannot be plainly proved from the Scriptures. Thus, there are but two necessary sacraments, Holy Baptism and the Holy Communion, because the great Head of the Church commanded these and these only for the Faithful. To be sure, the Church has other valuable sacraments that may rightfully be used, but they are minor in the sense that salvation does not depend on their use. Other characteristics of Anglicanism are its tradition of scholarship and its constant willingness to examine new truths as they are revealed by the Holy Spirit. In the light of these inherent traits it is probable that the Anglican Church has solved the relationship between faith and freedom more satisfactorily than has any other Christian Church: some Christian Churches have gained freedom for the individual at the expense of the whole faith, while others have kept the faith at the expense of freedom for the individual.

It is apparent that the Anglican Church also has an important contribution to make to the Ecumenical Movement, for by its patent inclusiveness it provides a nucleus for reuniting a large section of Christendom. This in itself faces Anglicans with a problem.

The Anglican Congress of 1954 issued a report from the Minneapolis meeting which said in part, ". . . we recommend that the Churches of the Anglican Communion take every opportunity for the building and strengthening of world-wide fellowship within our Communion." The Report went on to say: "We appeal to all the Churches of the Anglican Communion to strengthen their support of the Ecumenical Movement and to promote common action and the furthering of unity among Christians of different communions in their own local areas." [32] At first glance this dual directive appears to be completely contradictory, for any effort to strengthen our own unity might be done at the expense of our duty to the Ecumenical Movement, while any endeavor to take our place in the Ecumenical Movement might well tend to disrupt our own communion. This is the real dilemma which Anglicans must appreciate in order to understand their Church and her particular mission.

The unity of various Anglican Churches is maintained by a common faith expressed in the Book of Common Prayer, which is the standard of worship; by the historic episcopate, which is the standard and center of Church order; and by the fact that all the dioceses and provinces are in communion with the See of Canterbury. This represents a minimum of centripetal coherence necessary to hold so diverse a communion together, and indeed, it is likely that there should be some modification of the present principles of coherence if the Anglican Communion is to hold together.

The Anglican Church needs a common name, because such titles as "The Church of England in Australia and Tasmania," and "Nippon Sei Ko Kwai" are historically interesting, but quite confusing. As an illustration of commendable modification in this regard, "The Church of England in Canada" felicitously changed its name in 1955 to "The Anglican Church of Canada." It would be helpful if each province and diocese would make it clear in its legal title that it is a part of the Anglican Communion.

The Anglican Church needs also a common missionary strategy, which presupposes a permanent central staff, and planning on the highest inter-provincial level. This joint planning has but lately begun through the erection of the "Anglican Advisory Council on Missionary Strategy" at Lambeth in 1948. The Council held its first meeting in 1952, and it is supposed to meet every two years. While this is better than the former haphazard approach to the problem, it is obviously an inadequate solution for a task which calls for full-time staff work. Anglicans have made a fetish of decentralization, but American Churchmen could with propriety remind other Anglicans that just as the Articles of Confederation were not sufficiently strong to hold the former Colonies together, so the present loose system of Anglican cooperation calls for modification in the face of constant centrifugal forces.

Past duplication in missionary effort on the part of various Anglican provinces and missionary societies is still all too evident, and there are many areas which call for re-grouping. For instance, Cuba, Haiti, and the Dominican Republic might well be included in the Caribbean area of the present Province of the West Indies; Mexico, Central America, British Honduras, and Trinidad could form a separate province; and Liberia clearly belongs with the Province of West Africa rather than as an isolated missionary district of the American Church.

The total requirements and missionary opportunities of the entire world-wide communion need to be presented to all Anglicans so that they may see the true magnitude of the task to which God has called their Church. This might best be done through combined missionary planning and strategy as the expression of an organically united Anglican

Communion, the achievement of which would appear to be a primary task for our Church in this generation. Anglicans in many parts of the world have given much prayer, time, and thought towards reunion with other Christian bodies; and while this is commendable it is necessary that they give attention also to the needs of their own communion.

The Bishops at the 1948 Lambeth Conference spoke of their hopes for the reunion of Christendom, but in these cautionary words: "It is well to keep this vision before us; but we are still far from its attainment, and until this larger communion begins to take shape, it would be only a weakening of the present strength and service of the Anglican Communion if parts of it were severed from it prematurely. If we were slow to advance the larger cause it would be a betrayal of what we believe to be our special calling. It would be equally a betrayal of our trust before God, if the Anglican Communion were to allow itself to be dispersed before its particular work is done." [33]

A recent author has written in a similar warning vein concerning Anglicanism and the Ecumenical Movement: "If by any chance the Anglican Communion could not be held together, the clock would be set back five hundred years. If, on the other hand, we can maintain our position and prove that it is the source of vitally creative power, we shall by God's mercy perform a service of unique importance to Christendom and assist materially towards the fulfillment of our Lord's own prayer, 'ut omnes unum sint.' " [34]

The danger of dismemberment is a very real one because the Anglican Church is disparaged both by Roman Catholics and by many Protestants. The witness of the Episcopal Church in the United States and elsewhere is always in danger of being greatly weakened by the impact of an unyielding and supercilious Romanism on the one hand, and a powerful pan-Protestant organization on the other.

The Anglican Congress also called upon Anglicans everywhere to strengthen their support of the Ecumenical Movement, which has as its ultimate objective the reunion of Christendom, with the consequent disappearance of all denominational boundaries. Anglicans have taken an impressive part in the Ecumenical Movement during the last half-century; the names of Brent, Manning, Temple, Bell, Fisher, and Sherrill, and a host of others testify to the deep concern of our communion over this great "new fact of our time." Nor have the results been negligible, for Anglicans have full intercommunion with the Old Catholic Church, and with the Polish National Catholic Church; they have a measure of intercommunion with the Swedish National Church, and are a long step in the direction of full intercommunion with the Philippine Independent Church. In addition to these achievements, a number of Orthodox Churches have accepted the validity of Anglican Orders, in itself a significant step towards a more complete understanding with this large and influential section of Christendom.

In the field of Christian cooperation Anglican Churches have been members of the World Council of Churches since its formation in 1948, and have found it possible to work closely with other Christian bodies at international, national, and local levels. In one instance, four Anglican dioceses left their own communion to help form the Church of South India; a drastic step justifiable only if that Church is ultimately in communion with the See of Canterbury.

The Anglican Church has also supplied an important basis for reunion called the "Chicago-Lambeth Quadrilateral," a statement which has proved of great value in negotiations

206

with other Christian bodies. The American House of Bishops in putting forth the initial declaration in 1886 at Chicago said in part: "We do hereby affirm that the Christian unity now so earnestly desired . . . can be restored only by the return of all Christian communions to the principles of unity exemplified by the undivided Catholic Church during the first ages of its existence; which principles we believe to be the substantial deposit of Christian Faith and Order committed by Christ and His Apostles to the Church unto the end of the world, and therefore incapable of compromise or surrender by those who have been ordained to be its stewards and trustees for the common and equal benefit of all men." [35]

This "Quadrilateral", which the Lambeth Conference of 1888 adopted with modifications, states the terms upon which the Anglican Communion is willing to negotiate with other Christian bodies with a view to eventual reunion. In terms of the Church's faith they are: Belief in the Holy Scriptures of the Old and New Testaments as "containing all things necessary to salvation" and as being the "rule and ultimate standard of faith"; the Apostles' Creed as the "Baptismal symbol" and the Nicene Creed as "the sufficient statement of the Christian Faith"; the two Sacraments ordained by Christ Himself, Baptism and the Supper of the Lord, "ministered with unfailing use of Christ's words of Institution and of the elements ordered by Him";[36] and the historic episcopate "locally adapted in the methods of administration to the varying needs of the nations and peoples" who were called to the unity of the Church. This statement was the basic formula in the negotiations which led to the forming of the Church of South India.

It is apparent, then, that Anglicans face these two tasks: They must weld their own Church into an ever-closer unity, and they must also give informed and eager cooperation to the Ecumenical Movement. The Lambeth Conference of 1948 has a significant word to say on this point: "In our Resolutions, we recommend that in further schemes for reunion care should be taken to see that they do not, *unless for a brief time,** put any member of our family of Churches out of communion with it, and that they are not put into force unless after consultation with the rest of our family." [37] The weakness in this statement seems to lie in the words "unless for a brief time," for what are originally intended to be brief periods of history sometimes turn out to be of considerable duration.

Perhaps Anglicans would be better advised to determine that all future reunions with other Christian bodies, which involve Anglican provinces and dioceses, should be so devised that the united Church will immediately be in communion with the See of Canterbury.

Without doubt the Anglican Church has much to give to the cause of Christian reunion, since it contains within its own life a real and vital synthesis of both Catholic and Protestant Christianity. Anglicans who have this treasure must both hold it firmly, and offer it humbly to Christians at present in other communions, so that future reunions of Anglican provinces with other Christian bodies will be true to Catholic faith and order, as well as awake to the need for that continuing Biblical reappraisal of the Church which is a mark of true Evangelical Christianity.

* Italics mine.

Some Statistics on the Anglican Communion 1957

	Number of Dioceses	Baptized Membership
1 THE BRITISH ISLES		
The Church of England	43	20,000,000
The Church in Wales	6	750,000
The Church of Scotland	7	107,350
The Church of Ireland	14	480,000
		21,337,350
2 THE AMERICAS AND THE WEST INDIES		
The Protestant Episcopal Church	87	2,853,000
The Missionary District of Alaska	1	6,500
The Anglican Church of Canada	28	1,500,000
The Province of the West Indies	8	905,000
The Diocese of Bermuda	1	19,200
		5,283,700

The American Missionary Districts in the Caribbean,

	Number of Dioceses	Baptized Membership	
Mexico, and Central America:			
Cuba	1	59,000	
Haiti	1	57,000	
The Dominican Republic	1	4,000	
Puerto Rico	1	7,500	
The Virgin Islands	1	5,700	
Mexico	1	4,500	
Panama Canal Zone	1	22,000	
Central America	1	—	
			159,700
The Diocese of Argentina and eastern South America and the Falkland Islands	1	11,000	
The Missionary Districts of:			
Central Brazil	1	4,200	
Southern Brazil	1	16,000	
Southwestern Brazil	1	13,000	
			44,200

3 AFRICA

	Number of Dioceses	Baptized Membership
The Church of the Province of South Africa	14	1,100,000
The Province of Central Africa	4	161,400
The Dioceses of East Africa	7	900,000
The Province of West Africa	9	620,000
The Missionary District of Liberia	1	7,600
The Dioceses of:		
Egypt	1	n.s.a. —
North Africa	1	n.s.a. —
The Sudan	1	38,000

	Number of Dioceses	Baptized Membership	
Mauritius and The Seychelles	1	6,000	
Madagascar	1	30,000	
			2,863,000

4 INDIA, PAKISTAN, BURMA, AND CEYLON; THE EAST INDIES

	Number of Dioceses	Baptized Membership	
The Church of India, Pakistan, Burma, and Ceylon	15	350,000	
Borneo	1	20,000	
Singapore	1	21,000	
			391,000

5 AUSTRALASIA

	Number of Dioceses	Baptized Membership	
The Church of England in Australia and Tasmania	25	3,000,000	
The Province of New Zealand	9	781,000	
			3,781,000

6 THE FAR EAST

	Number of Dioceses	Baptized Membership	
The Holy Catholic Church in China	14	42,000	
The Diocese of Victoria—Hong Kong	1	n.s.a.	
The Holy Catholic Church in Japan	10	40,000	
The Diocese of Korea	1	5,000	
The Missionary District of the Philippines	1	33,300	
The Missionary District of Honolulu and Okinawa	1	17,300	
			137,600

	Number of Dioceses	Baptized Membership
7 EUROPE AND THE NEAR EAST		
North and Central Europe	1	1,700
Gibraltar	1	—
American Convocations in Europe		1,700
The Archbishopric of Jerusalem	1	15,000
The Diocese of Jordan, Syria, and Lebanon	1	n.s.a.
The Diocese of Iran	1	1,500
Total Number of Dioceses	331	19,900
Estimated Total Baptized Members		34,017,450

Author's Notes

1 Letter from Archbishop Benson to Archbishop Maclagan, October 11, 1896. Quoted in How, F. D., *Archbishop Maclagan* (London: Wells Gardner, 1912), p. 351.

2 The dates when various Orthodox Churches declared themselves willing to accept the validity of Anglican ordinations are: Constantinople, 1922; Jerusalem and Cyprus, 1923; Alexandria, 1930; Roumania, 1936; Greece, 1939. It must be understood that this recognition is only conditional for it would take an Ecumenical Council to ratify these declarations.

3 *Lambeth Conference Report.* 1930, pp. 48-55 from Resolution #49.

4 Quoted by Alfred Barry, *The Ecclesiastical Expansion of England*, p. 6.

5 Malden, R. H., *The English Church and Nation*, p. 264.

6 Boswell, James, *Life of Johnson* (Oxford, 1922), I, 310.

7 Barry Alfred, *op. cit.*, p. 92.

8 Curtis, W. R., *The Lambeth Conferences*, p. 64.

9 Curtis, W. R., *ibid.*, p. 127.

10 Malden, R. H., *op. cit.* p. 277.

11 Morehouse, C. P., *The Episcopal Church Annual*, 1957, p. 23.

12 Latourette, K. S., *A History of the Expansion of Christianity*, IV, 256 and 311.

13 Quoted in *The Living Church,* November 16, 1947.

14 *Pan-Anglican,* October, 1955, p. 48.

15 *Ibid.,* October, 1951, p. 56.

16 Wand, J. W. C., *The Anglican Communion,* p. 235.

17 *Pan-Anglican,* Easter, 1952, p. 5.

18 Pascoe, C. F., *Two Hundred Years of the S. P. G., 1701-1900,* p. 399.

19 Gwyther, J., *Captain Cook and the South Pacific* (Cambridge, 1954), p. 161.

20 Latourette, K. S., *op. cit.,* V, 137.

21 Creighton, L., *George Augustus Selwyn,* p. 132.

22 *Pan-Anglican,* Easter, 1955, p. 19.

23 Creighton, L., *op. cit.,* p. 130.

24 *Proceedings of the Board of Missions, Episcopal Church,* 1836, p. 94; 1837, p. 94.

25 Schereschewsky was the fourth Jewish Christian to be consecrated an Anglican bishop. Others were: Michael Solomon Alexander, Jerusalem, 1841; Isaac Helmuth, Huron, 1871; John Gottlieb Auer, Cape Palmas (Liberia), 1873.

26 Latourette, K. S., *op. cit.,* VI, 364.

27 *Church Times,* Jan. 14, 1955, August 10, 1956. *The Living Church,* July 15, 1956.

28. Tucker, H. St. G., *History of the Episcopal Church in Japan,* p. 2.

29 *Japan Missions,* Autumn, 1955, p. 3.

30 Whipple, H. B., *Lights and Shadows of a Long Episcopate* (London, 1899), p. 339.

31 *Handbook of the Anglican Bishopric in Jerusalem and the East* (Jerusalem, 1941).

32 *Anglican Congress* (Greenwich, Connecticut: Seabury Press, 1954), p. 196.

33 *Lambeth Conference Report, 1948* (London: S.P.C.K., 1948) , p. 23.

34 Wand, J. W. C., *op. cit.,* p. 331.

35 Report of the Committee on Christian Unity, Adopted and Set Forth by the House of Bishops as an Official Declaration, October 20, 1886, at Chicago.

36 Malden, R. H., *op. cit.,* p. 327.

37 *Lambeth Conference Report, 1948,* p. 23.

Bibliography

GENERAL READING

Addison, J. T., *Our Expanding Church*. New York: National Council, Episcopal Church, 1930.

Allen, W. O. B., and McClure, E., *Two Hundred Years: The History of the S.P.C.K., 1698-1898*. London: S.P.C.K., 1898.

Barry, A., *The Ecclesiastical Expansion of England*. London: Macmillan, 1895.

Campbell, J. McL., *Christian History in the Making*. London: Press & Publications Board, 1946.

Dart, J. L. C., *The Old Reiigion*. London: S.P.C.K., 1956.

Gray, W. H., Ed., *Pan-Anglican*. Published semi-annually from 1950, by Church Missions Publishing Company, Hartford, Conn.

Jenkins, C., and Mackenzie, K. D., *Episcopacy Ancient and Modern*. London: S.P.C.K., 1930.

Latourette, K. S., *A History of the Expansion of Christianity*. 7 v. New York: Harper, 1941.

Pascoe, C. F., *Two Hundred Years of the S.P.G.* London: S.P.G., 1901.

Stock, E., *History of the Church Missionary Society*. 3 v. London: C.M.S., 1899.

Thompson, H. P., *Into All Lands. History of S.P.G., 1701-1950*. London: S.P.G., 1951.

Wand, J. W. C. (Ed.), *The Anglican Communion*. London: Oxford, 1948.

CHAPTER I

THE BRITISH ISLES

The Church of England

Bell, G. K. A., *A Brief Sketch of the Church of England.* London: Hodder & Stoughton, 1948.

Curtis, W. R., *The Lambeth Conferences.* New York: Columbia University, 1942.

Garbett, C., *The Claims of the Church of England.* London: Hodder & Stoughton, 1947.

Malden, R. H., *The English Church and Nation.* London: S.P.C.K., 1952.

Moorman, J. R. H., *A History of the Church in England.* New York: Morehouse-Gorham, 1954.

Edwards, A. G., *Landmarks in the History of the Welsh Church.* London: John Murray, 1912.

James, J. W., *A Church History of Wales.* Ilfracombe: A. H. Stockwell, 1945.

Goldie, F., *A Short History of the Episcopal Church in Scotland.* London: S.P.C.K., 1951.

Luckock, H. M., *The Church in Scotland.* London: Wells Gardner, 1893.

Mitchell, A., *Scotland's Church.* Dundee: David Winter, 1933.

Bland, F. E., *How the Church Missionary Society Came to Ireland.* Dublin: Church of Ireland Publishing Company, 1935.

Holloway, H., *The Reformation in Ireland.* London: S.P.C.K., 1919.

Phillips, W. A., *History of the Church of Ireland.* 3 v. London: Oxford University, 1933.

CHAPTER II

THE AMERICAS AND THE WEST INDIES

*The Protestant Episcopal Church
in the United States of America*

Chorley, E. C., *Men and Movements in the American Episcopal Church*. New York: Scribner's, 1946.

Manross, W. W., *A History of the American Episcopal Church*. New York: Morehouse-Gorham, 1935.

Morehouse, F. C., *Some American Churchmen*. Milwaukee: Young Churchman, 1892.

Smith, L. C., *Life of Philander Chase*. New York: Dutton, 1903.

Stowe, W. H., Ed., *Historical Magazine*. A Quarterly published by the Church Historical Society, New Brunswick, New Jersey.

Tuttle, D. S., *Reminiscences of a Missionary Bishop*. New York: T. Whittaker, 1906.

White, G., *An Apostle of the Western Church: Jackson Kemper*. New York: T. Whittaker, 1899.

The District of Alaska

Jenkins, T., *Man of Alaska* (P. T. Rowe). New York: Morehouse-Gorham, 1943.

The Anglican Church of Canada

Cody, H. A., *William Carpenter Bompas*. New York: E. P. Dutton, 1913.

Fleming, A. L., *Archibald the Arctic*. New York: Appleton, 1956.

Langtry, J., *History of the Church in Eastern Canada and Newfoundland*. London: S.P.C.K., 1892.

Lydekker, J. W., *Life and Letters of Charles Inglis*. London: S.P.C.K., 1936.

Machray, R., *Life of Robert Machray*. Toronto: Macmillan, 1909.

Tucker, H. W., *Memoirs of the Life and Episcopate of Edward Feild*. London: W. Wells Gardner, 1877.

Vernon, C. W., *The Old Church in the New Dominion*. London: S.P.C.K., 1929.

The Church of the Province of the West Indies

Caldecott, A., *The Church in the West Indies*. London: S.P.C.K., 1898.

Ellis, J. B., *The Diocese of Jamaica*. London: S.P.C.K., 1913.

Farrar, T., *Notes on the History of the Church in Jamaica*. Berbice: McDonald, 1892.

The Districts of Cuba; Haiti and the Dominican Republic; Puerto Rico and the Virgin Islands; Mexico; The Canal Zone; Central America

————, *Eden of the Americas*. New York: National Council, Episcopal Church.

————, *Land of Contrasts*. New York: National Council, Episcopal Church.

————, *The West Indies*, No. V Handbooks of the Missions of the Episcopal Church. New York: National Council, Episcopal Church.

Camargo, G. B., and Grubb, K. G., *Religion in the Republic of Mexico*. London: World Dominion Press, 1935.

Creighton, F. W., *The Church in Mexico*. New York: National Council, 1929.

————, *Mexico*. New York: National Council, 1936.

Bury, H., *A Bishop Amongst Bananas.* Milwaukee: Young Churchman Company, 1911.

The Diocese of Argentina and Eastern South America with the Falkland Islands; The Districts of Central, Southern, and Southwestern Brazil

Every, E. F., *The Anglican Church in South America.* London: S.P.C.K., 1915.

Macdonald, F. C., *Bishop Stirling of the Falklands.* London: Serley Service, 1929.

Pride, A., and Cowell, A. J., *South America:* A Handbook of the Work of the South American Missionary Society. London: S.A.M.S., n.d.

CHAPTER III

AFRICA

The Province of South Africa

Agar-Hamilton, J. A. I., *A Transvaal Jubilee.* London: S.P.C.K., 1928.

Brooke, A., *Robert Gray.* London: Oxford, 1947.

Gray, C., *Life of Robert Gray.* 2 v. London: Rivington, 1876.

Lewis, C. and Edwards, G. E., *Historical Records of the Church of the Province of South Africa.* London: S.P.C.K., 1934.

Marquard, L., *The Peoples and Policies of South Africa.* New York: Oxford, 1952.

Osmund, V., *The Salient of South Africa.* London: S.P.C.K., 1931.

The Province of Central Africa

Barnes, B. H., *Johnson of Nyasaland*. London: U.M.C.A., 1933.

Heanley, R. M., *A Memoir of Edward Steere*. London: U.M.C.A., 1898.

Ward, G., *The Life of Charles Alan Smythies*. London: U.M.C.A., 1899.

Wilson, G. H., *The History of the Universities Mission to Central Africa*. London: U.M.C.A., 1936.

The Dioceses of East Africa

Dawson, E. C., *James Hannington*. London: Randolph, 1886.

Hole, C., *The Early History of the Church Missionary Society to 1814*. London: C.M.S., 1896.

Smith, H. M., *Frank Weston*. London: Longmans, 1926.

Tucker, A. R., *Eighteen Years in Uganda and East Africa*. 2 v. London: Arnold, 1908.

The Province of West Africa

Page, J., *Samuel Crowther*. New York: Revell, 1889.

Walker, F. D., *The Romance of the Black River*. London: C.M.S., 1930.

Madagascar

McMahon, E. O., *Christian Missions in Madagascar*. Westminster: S.P.C.K., 1914.

Webster, A. N., *Madagascar*. London: S.P.G., 1932.

CHAPTER IV

INDIA, PAKISTAN, BURMA, AND CEYLON; THE EAST INDIES

The Church of India, Pakistan, Burma, and Ceylon

Ashley-Brown, W., *On the Bombay Coast and Deccan.* London: S.P.C.K., 1937.

Bateman, J., *Daniel Wilson.* 2 v. Boston: Gould & Lincoln, 1860.

Chatterton, E., *A History of the Church of England in India.* London: S.P.C.K., 1929.

Cotton, (Mrs.) G. E. L., *Bishop G. E. L. Cotton.* London, 1871.

Graham, C., *Azariah of Dornakal.* London: S.C.M., 1946.

Neill, S., *Out of Bondage.* London: Edinburgh House Press, 1930.

Padwick, C. E., *Henry Martyn.* New York: Doran, 1923.

Smith, G., *Reginald Heber.* London: J. Murray, 1895.

The Diocese of Borneo

Baring-Gould, S. and Bampfylde, C. A., *A History of Sarawak under the Two White Rajahs, 1839-1908.* London: H. Sotheran, 1909.

Bunyon, C. G., *Memoirs of Bishop McDougall.* London: Longmans, 1889.

CHAPTER V

AUSTRALASIA

The Church of England in Australia and Tasmania

Alexander, F. (Ed.), *Four Bishops and Their See.* Nedlands, W. A.: Univ. of Western Australia, 1957.

Boodle, R. G., *The Life and Labours of the Rt. Rev. William Tyrrell.* London: Wells Gardner, 1881.

Henrich, R., *South Sea Epic.* London: S.P.G., 1944.

Johnstone, S. M., *A History of the C.M.S. in Australia and Tasmania.* Sydney: C.M.S., 1925.

Ramsden, E., *Marsden and the Mission.* Sydney: Angus & Robertson, 1936.

White, G., *Round About the Torres Straits.* London: S.P.C.K., 1925.

Whitington, F. T., *William Grant Broughton.* Sydney: Angus & Robertson, 1936.

The Province of New Zealand

Creighton, L., *J. A. Selwyn.* London: Longmans, 1923.

How, F. D., *Bishop John Selwyn.* London: Isbister, 1899.

Jacobs, H., *New Zealand.* London: S.P.C.K., 1887.

Johnstone, S. M., *Samuel Marsden.* Sydney: Angus & Robertson, 1932.

Paton, F. H. L., *Patteson of Melanesia.* London: S.P.C.K., 1930.

Purchas, H. T., *A History of the English Church in New Zealand.* Christ Church, N.Z.: Simpson & Williams, 1914.

Tucker, H. W., *Memoir of the Life and Episcopate of George Augustus Selwyn.* 2 v. New York: Pott Young, 1879.

Williams, W., *Christianity Among the New Zealanders.* London: Seeley Jackson Halliday, 1868.

Yonge, C. M., *Bishop John Coleridge Patteson.* 2 v. London: Macmillan, 1874.

CHAPTER VI

THE FAR EAST

The Holy Catholic Church in China

Huntington, V. E., *Along the Great River*. New York: National Council, Episcopal Church, 1940.

Latourette, K. S., *A History of Christian Missions in China*. New York: Macmillan, 1929.

Muller, J. A., *Apostle of China: Schereschewsky*. New York: Morehouse-Gorham, 1937.

Pakenham-Walsh, W. S., *Twenty Years in China*. Cambridge: W. Heffer, 1935.

Richmond, A. B., *The American Episcopal Church in China*. New York: National Council (Episcopal), 1907.

The Holy Catholic Church in Japan

Bickersteth, S., *Life and Letters of Edward Bickersteth*. London: Sampson, Low, Marston, 1899.

Carey, O., *A History of Christianity in Japan*. 2 v. New York: Revell, 1909.

Robbins, H. C., and McNaught, G. K., *Dr. Rudolph Bolling Teusler*. New York: Scribner's, 1942.

Sansbury, C. K., *Japan*. London: S.P.G., 1947.

Tucker, H. St. G., *The History of the Episcopal Church in Japan*. New York: Scribner's, 1938.

The Diocese of Korea

Trollope, C., *Mark Napier Trollope*. London: S.P.C.K., 1936.

Trollope, M. N., *The Church in Korea*. London: Mowbray, 1915.

The Philippine Episcopal Church

Gowen, V. H., *Philippine Kaleidoscope*. New York: National Council, Episcopal Church.

Zabriskie, A. C., *Bishop Brent: Crusader for Christian Unity*. Philadelphia: Westminster, 1948.

The District of Honolulu

Restarick, H. B., *Hawaii, 1778-1920*. Honolulu, 1924.

CHAPTER VII

EUROPE AND THE NEAR EAST

North and Central Europe

Mason, A. J., *William Edward Collins, Bishop of Gibraltar*. New York: Longmans, 1912.

The Bishop in Jerusalem

Gobat, S., *Samuel Gobat, Bishop of Jerusalem*. New York: T. Whittaker, 1885.

————, *Handbook of the Anglican Bishops in Jerusalem* (1941).